PAPER BACK LYRICS

COMPLETE LYRICS FOR OVER 145 SONGS

The
1980s

HAL•LEONARD®

ISBN 13: 978-1-4234-1195-6
ISBN 10: 1-4234-1195-1

HAL•LEONARD®
CORPORATION

7777 W. BLUEMOUND RD. P.O. BOX 13819 MILWAUKEE, WI 53213

Visit Hal Leonard Online at
www.halleonard.com

CONTENTS

Africa

Words and Music by David Paich and Jeff Porcaro

recorded by Toto

I hear the drums echoin' tonight.
She hears only whispers of some quiet conversation.
She's coming in, twelve-thirty flight.
Moonlit wings reflect the stars that guide me toward salvation.
I stopped an old man along the way,
Hoping to find some old forgotten words or ancient melodies.
He turned to me as if to say,
"Hurry, boy, it's waiting there for you."

It's gonna take a lot to drag me away from you.
There's nothing that a hundred men or more could ever do.
I bless the rains down in Africa.
Gonna take some time to do the things we never had.

The wild dogs cry out in the night.
As they grow restless, longing for some solitary company.
I know that I must do what's right,
Sure as Kilimanjaro rises like Olympus above the Serengeti.
I seem to cure what's deep inside,
Frightened of this thing that I've become.

It's gonna take a lot to drag me away from you.
There's nothing that a hundred men or more could ever do.
I bless the rains down in Africa.
Gonna take some time to do the things we never had.

All I Need Is a Miracle

Words and Music by Mike Rutherford and Christopher Neil

recorded by Mike & The Mechanics

I said go if you wanna go,
Stay if you wanna stay.
I didn't care if you hung around me,
I didn't care if you went away.
And I know you were never right;
I'll admit I was never wrong.
I could never make up my mind,
I made it up as I went along.
And though I treated you like a child,
I'm gonna miss you for the rest of my life.

Refrain:
All I need is a miracle. All I need is you.
All I need is a miracle. All I need is you.
All I need is a miracle. All I need is you.

I never had any time,
And I never had any call,
But I went out of my way just to hurt you
The one I shouldn't hurt at all.
I thought I was being cool;
Yeah, I thought I was being strong.
But it's always the same old story,
You never know what you've got till it's gone.
If I ever catch up with you
I'm gonna love you for the rest of your life.

Refrain

And if I ever catch up with you
I'm gonna love you for the rest of your life.

Refrain

Against All Odds
(Take a Look at Me Now)

Words and Music by Phil Collins

from the film *Against All Odds*
recorded by Phil Collins

How can I just let you walk away,
Just let you leave without a trace?
When I stand here taking
Every breath with you,
You're the only one
Who really knows me at all.

How can you just walk away from me,
When all I can do is watch you leave.
'Cause we've shared the laughter and the pain,
And even shared the tears.
You're the only one who really knew me at all.

So take a look at me now
'Cause there's just an empty space.
There's nothing left here to remind me,
Just the memory of your face.
So take a look at me now,
There's just an empty space,
And you coming back to me is against the odds,
And that's what I've got to face.

I wish I could just make you turn around,
Turn around and see me cry.
There's so much I need to say to you,
So many reasons why
You're the only one who really knew me at all.

So take a look at me now,
There's just an empty space,
And there's nothing left here to remind me,
Just the memory of your face.
So take a look at me now,
'Cause there's just an empty space.
But to wait for you is all I can do,
And that's what I've got to face.

Take a good look at me now
'Cause I'll still be standing here,
And you coming back to me is against all odds.
That's the chance I've got to take... Take a look at me now.

Against the Wind

Words and Music by Bob Seger

recorded by Bob Seger & The Silver Bullet Band

It seems like yesterday, but it was long ago.
Janey was lovely. She was the queen of my nights,
There in the darkness with the radio playin' low,
And the secrets that we shared, the mountains that we moved,
Caught like a wild fire out of control
Till there was nothin' left to burn and nothin' left to prove.
And I remember what she said to me, how she swore that it never
    would end.
I remember how she held me oh so tight,
Wish I didn't know now what I didn't know then.
Against the wind, we were runnin' against the wind.
We were young and strong, we were runnin' against the wind.

And the years rolled slowly past. And I found myself alone,
Surrounded by strangers I thought were my friends.
I found myself further and further from my home, and I guess I lost
    my way.
There were oh so many roads. I was livin' to run and runnin' to live.
Never worried about payin', or even how much I owed.
Movin' eight miles a minute for months at a time, breakin' all of the
    rules that would bend,
I began to find myself searchin', searchin' for shelter again and again.
Against the wind, little somethin' against the wind.
I found myself seekin' shelter against the wind.

Well, those drifter's days are past me now.
I've got so much to think about: deadlines and commitments,
What to leave in, what to leave out.
Against the wind, I'm still runnin' against the wind.
I'm older now, but still runnin' against the wind.
Well, I'm older now, and still runnin' against the wind,
Against the wind.

All Out of Love

Words and Music by Graham Russell and Clive Davis

recorded by Air Supply

I'm lying alone with my head on the phone,
Thinking of you 'til it hurts.
I know you hurt too, but what else can we do,
Tormented and torn apart.

I wish I could carry your smile in my heart,
For times when my life feels so low.
It would make me believe what tomorrow could bring,
When today doesn't really know, doesn't really know.

Refrain:
I'm all out of love, I'm so lost without you,
I know you were right, believing for so long.
I'm all out of love, what am I without you?
I can't be too late to say that I was so wrong.

I want you to come back and carry me home,
Away from these long, lonely nights.
I'm reaching for you. Are you feeling it too?
Does the feeling seem oh, so right?

And what would you say if I called on you now,
And said that I can't hold on?
There's no easy way, it gets harder each day,
Please love me or I'll be gone, I'll be gone.

Refrain

Ooh, what are you thinking of?
What are you thinking of?
What are you thinking of?
What are you thinking of?

Refrain

Almost Paradise

Words by Dean Pitchford
Music by Eric Carmen

Love Theme from the Paramount Motion Picture *Footloose*
from the Broadway Musical *Footloose*
recorded by Mike Reno & Ann Wilson

Ren:
I thought that dreams belonged to other men,
'Cause each time I got close, they'd fall apart again.
Ariel:
I feared my heart would beat in secrecy.
Both:
I faced the nights alone.
Oh, how could I have known
That all my life I only needed you?

Refrain:
Whoa, almost paradise,
We're knockin' on heaven's door.
Almost paradise,
How could we ask for more?
I swear that I can see forever in your eyes.
Paradise.

Ariel:
I thought that perfect love was hard to find.
I'd almost given up; you must have read my mind.
Ren:
And all those dreams I saved for a rainy day,
Ariel:
Ooh, they're finally coming true.
I'll share them all with you,
'Cause now we hold the future in our hands.

Refrain

Ren:
And in your arms salvation's not so far away.
Ariel:
It's getting closer, closer every day.

Refrain

Paradise. Paradise.

Alone

Words and Music by Billy Steinberg and Tom Kelly

recorded by Heart

I hear the ticking of the clock;
I'm lying here, the room's pitch dark.
I wonder where you are tonight,
No answer on the telephone.
And the night goes by so very slow,
Oh, I hope that it won't end, though,
Alone.

Refrain:
'Til now I always got by on my own,
I never really cared until I met you.
And now it chills me to the bone.
How do I get you alone?
How do I get you alone?

You don't know how long I have wanted
To touch your lips and hold you tight.
You don't know how long I have waited,
And I was gonna tell you tonight.
But the secret is still my own,
And my love for you is still unknown,
Alone.

Refrain

How do I get you alone?
How do I get you alone, alone, alone?

Always on My Mind

Words and Music by Wayne Thompson, Mark James and Johnny Christopher

recorded by Willie Nelson, The Pet Shop Boys

Maybe I didn't treat you
Quite as good as I should have.
Maybe I didn't love you,
Quite as often as I should have;
Little things I should have said and done,
I just never took the time.

Tell me,
Tell me that your sweet love hasn't died.
Give me,
Give me one more chance to keep you satisfied, satisfied.

Maybe I didn't hold you,
All those lonely, lonely times;
And I guess I never told you
I'm so happy that you're mine.
If I made you feel second best,
Girl, I'm sorry I was blind.

You were always on my mind;
You were always on my mind.

You were always on my mind;
You were always on my mind.

Amanda

Words and Music by Tom Scholz

recorded by Boston

Babe, tomorrow's so far away.
There's somethin' I just have to say
I don't think I could hide
What I'm feelin' inside another day
Knowin' I love you.

And I, I'm gettin' too close again.
I don't wanna see it end.
If I tell you tonight,
Will you turn out the light and walk away
Knowin' I love you?

I'm gonna take you by surprise
And make you realize, Amanda.
I'm gonna tell you right away;
I can't wait another day, Amanda.
I'm gonna say it like a man
And make you understand, Amanda.
I love you.

And I feel like today's the day.
I'm lookin' for the words to say.
Do you wanna be free?
Are you ready for me to feel this way?
I don't wanna lose ya.

So, it may be too soon, I know.
The feelin' takes so long to grow.
If I tell you today
Will you turn me away and let me go?
I don't wanna lose you.

I'm gonna take you by surprise
And make you realize, Amanda.
I'm gonna tell you right away;
I can't wait another day, Amanda.
I'm gonna say it like a man
And make you understand, Amanda.
Oh, girl.

You and I, I know that we can't wait.
And I swear, I swear it's not a lie, girl.
Tomorrow may be too late.
You, you and I, girl, we can share a life together.
It's now or never, and tomorrow may be too late. Oh.

And feelin' the way I do,
I don't wanna wait my whole life through
To say I'm in love with you.

America

Words and Music by Neil Diamond

from the motion picture *The Jazz Singer*
recorded by Neil Diamond

Far, we've been traveling far
Without a home, but not without a star
Free, only want to be free
We huddle close, hang on to a dream

On the boats and on the planes
They're coming to America
Never looking back again
They're coming to America

Home, don't it seem so far away
Oh, we're traveling light today
In the eye of the storm
In the eye of the storm

Home to a new and a shiny place
Make our bed, and we'll say our grace
Freedom's light burning warm
Freedom's light burning warm

Ev'rywhere around the world
They're coming to America
Ev'ry time that flag's unfurled
They're coming to America

Got a dream to take them there
They're coming to America
Got a dream, they've come to share
They're coming to America

They're coming to America
They're coming to America
They're coming to America
They're coming to America today,
Today, today, today, today

My country, 'tis of thee (today)
Sweet land of liberty (today)
Of thee I sing (today)
Of thee I sing today

Repeat and Fade:
Today, today

Another One Bites the Dust

Words and Music by John Deacon

recorded by Queen

Steve walks warily down the street
With the brim pulled way down low.
Ain't no sound but the sound of his feet;
Machine guns ready to go.
Are you ready, hey! Are you ready for this?
Are you hanging on the edge of your seat?
Out of the doorway the bullets rip
To the sound of the beat.

Refrain:
Another one bites the dust.
Another one bites the dust.
And another one gone,
And another one gone.
Another one bites the dust.
Hey! I'm gonna get you too.
Another one bites the dust.

How do you think I'm going to get along
Without you when you're gone?
You took me for ev'rything that I had
And kicked me out on my own.
Are you happy? Are you satisfied?
How long can you stand the heat?
Out of the doorway the bullets rip
To the sound of the beat.

Refrain

Four Times:
Another one bites the dust.

There are plenty of ways that you can hurt a man
And bring him to the ground.
You can beat him, you can cheat him, you can treat him bad,
And leave him when he's down.
But I'm ready, yes, I'm ready for you.
I'm standing on my own two feet.
Out of the doorway the bullets rip
To the sound of the beat.

Refrain

Back in the High Life Again

Words and Music by Will Jennings and Steve Winwood

recorded by Steve Winwood

It used to seem to me that my life ran on too fast,
And I had to take it slowly
Just to make the good parts last.
But when you're born to run,
It's so hard to just slow down,
So don't be surprised to see me
Back in that bright part of town.

I'll be back in the high life again.
All the doors I closed one time will open up again.
I'll be back in the high life again.
All the eyes that watched me once will smile and take me in.
And I'll drink and dance with one hand free,
Let the world back into me.
And oh, I'll be a sight to see,
Back in the high life again.

You used to be the best to make life be life to me,
And I hope that you're still out there.
And you're like you used to be.
We'll have ourselves a time,
And we'll dance till the morning sun,
And we'll let the good times come in
And we won't stop until we're done.

Refrain (Twice):
We'll be back in the high life again.
All the doors I closed one time will open up again.
We'll be back in the high life again.
All the eyes that watched us once will smile and take us in.
And we'll drink and dance with one hand free,
And have the world so easily.
And oh, we'll be a sight to see,
Back in the high life again.

High life.
Back in the high life.
Oh, we'll be back.

The Best of Times

Words and Music by Dennis DeYoung

recorded by Styx

Tonight's the night we'll make history;
Honey, you and I;
'Cause I'll take any risk to tie back the hands of time,
And stay with you here tonight.

I know you feel these are the worst of times;
I do believe it's true.
When people lock their doors and hide inside;
Rumor has it, it's the end of paradise;
But I know if the world just passed us by, baby,
I know I wouldn't have to cry, no, no.

The best of times are when I'm alone with you;
Some rain, some shine; we'll make this a world for two.
Our memories of yesterday will last a lifetime.
We'll take the best, forget the rest,
And someday we'll find these are the best of times.
These are the best of times.

The headlines read these are the worst of times;
I do believe it's true.
I feel so helpless, like a boat against the tide;
I wish the summer winds could bring back paradise;
But I know if the world turned upside down, baby,
I know you'd always be around, my, my.

Repeat and Fade:
The best of times are when I'm alone with you;
Some rain, some shine; we'll make this a world for two.

Brass in Pocket

Words and Music by Chrissie Hynde and James Honeyman-Scott

recorded by The Pretenders

Got brass in pocket,
Got bottle, I'm gonna use it.
Intention, I feel inventive,
Gonna make you, make you, make you notice.

Got motion, restrained emotion.
Been driving, Detroit leaning.
No reason it seems so pleasing.
Gonna make you, make you, make you notice.

Refrain:
Gonna use my arms,
Gonna use my legs,
Gonna use my style,
Gonna use my side-step,
Gonna use my fingers.
Gonna use my, my, my imagination,
'Cause I gonna make you see
There's nobody else here, no one like me.
I'm special, so special.
I gotta have some of your attention, give it to me.

Got rhythm, I can't miss a beat.
I got new skank so reet.
Got something, I'm winking at you.
Gonna make you, make you, make you notice.

Refrain

Oh, oh, oh, and when you walk.

Call Me

Words by Deborah Harry
Music by Giorgio Moroder

from the Paramount Motion Picture *American Gigolo*
recorded by Blondie

Color me your color, baby, color me your car.
Color me your color, darling, I know who you are.
Come up off your color chart,
I know where you're coming from.
Call me on the line,
Call me any, any time.
Call me, I love you,
Can't you call me any day or night.

Candle in the Wind

Music by Elton John
Words by Bernie Taupin

recorded by Elton John

Goodbye, Norma Jean, though I never knew you at all
You had the grace to hold yourself while those around you crawled.
They crawled out of the woodwork and they whispered into you brain.
They set you on the treadmill and they made you change your name.

Refrain:
It seems to me you lived your life like a candle in the wind,
Never knowing who to cling to when the rain set in.
I would have liked to have known you, but I was just a kid.
Your candle burned out long before your legend ever did.

Loneliness was tough, the toughest role you ever played.
Hollywood created a superstar and pain was the price you paid.
Even when you died, oh, the press still hounded you.
All the papers had to say was that Marilyn was found in the nude.

Refrain

Goodbye, Norma Jean, though I never knew you at all
You had the grace to hold yourself while those around you crawled.
Goodbye, Norma Jean, from a young man in the twenty second row
Who sees you as something more than sexual,
    more than just Marilyn Monroe.

Refrain

I would have liked to have known you, whoa, but I was just a kid.
Your candle burned out long before your legend ever did.

Can't Fight This Feeling

Words and Music by Kevin Cronin

recorded by REO Speedwagon

I can't fight this feelin' any longer,
And yet I'm still afraid to let it flow.
What started out as friendship has grown stronger;
I only wish I had the strength to let it show.

I tell myself that I can't hold out forever.
I say there is no reason for my fear,
'Cause I feel so secure when we're together.
You give my life direction. You make ev'rything so clear.

And even as I wander, I'm keepin' you in sight.
You're a candle in the window on a cold, dark winter's night.
And I'm getting closer than I ever thought I might.
And I can't fight this feelin' anymore.

I've forgotten what I started fightin' for.
It's time to bring this ship into the shore
And throw away the oars forever.
'Cause I can't fight this feelin' anymore.

I've forgotten what I started fightin' for.
And if I have to crawl upon the floor,
Come crashin' through your door, baby,
I can't fight this feelin' anymore.

My life has been such a whirlwind since I saw you.
I've been runnin' around in circles in my mind.
And it always seems that I'm followin' you, girl,
'Cause you take me to the places that alone I'd never find.

And even as I wander, I'm keepin' you in sight.
You're a candle in the window on a cold, dark winter's night.
And I'm getting closer than I ever thought I might.
And I can't fight this feelin' anymore.

I've forgotten what I started fightin' for.
It's time to bring this ship into the shore
And throw away the oars forever.
'Cause I can't fight this feelin' anymore.

I've forgotten what I started fightin' for.
And if I have to crawl upon the floor,
Come crashin' through your door, baby,
I can't fight this feelin' anymore.

Centerfold

Written by Seth Justman

recorded by J. Geils Band

Does she walk? Does she talk?
Does she come complete?
My homeroom, homeroom angel,
Always pulled me from my seat.
She was pure like snowflakes;
No one could ever stain the memory of my angel,
Could never cause me pain.
The years go by, I'm lookin' through a girlie magazine,
And there's my homeroom angel On the pages in between.

Refrain:
My blood runs cold;
My memory has just been sold.
My angel is the centerfold.
Angel is the centerfold.
My blood runs cold;
My memory has just been sold.
Angel in the centerfold.

Slipped me notes under the desk
While I was thinkin' about her dress.
I was shy, I turned away
Before she caught my eye.

I was shakin' in my shoes
Whenever she flashed those baby blues.
Something had a hold on me,
When angel passed close by.
Those soft fuzzy sweaters too magical to touch!
To see her in that negligee is really just too much!

Refrain

It's okay, I understand,
This ain't no never, never land.
I hope that when this issue's gone,
I'll see you when your clothes are on.
Take your car, yes we will,
We'll take your car and drive it.
We'll take it to a motel room and take 'emoff in private.
A part of me had been ripped,
The pages from my mind are stripped,
Ay no! I can't deny it. Oh yeah, I guess I gotta buy it.

Refrain

Na na na na…

The Closer You Get

Words and Music by James Pennington and Mark Gray

recorded by Alabama

Refrain:
The closer you get, the further I fall,
I'll be over the edge now in no time at all.
I'm falling faster and faster and faster with no time to stall.
The closer you get, the further I fall.

The things that you say to me,
The look on your face,
Brings out the man in me.
Do I see a trace in your eyes of love?

Refrain

Could I be dreaming?
Is this really real?
'Cause there's something magic
The way I feel in your arms tonight.

Refrain

Keep fallin', oh, yeah, yeah.
Keep fallin',
Mm, fallin', oh, yeah, yeah,
I'm fallin'.

Coming Around Again

Words and Music by Carly Simon

from the Paramount Picture *Heartburn*
recorded by Carly Simon

Baby sneezes, Mommy pleases,
Daddy breezes in.
So good on paper, so romantic,
But so bewildering.

Refrain:
I know nothing stays the same,
But if you're willing to play the game,
It's coming around again.
So don't mind if I fall apart;
There's more room in a broken heart.

You pay the grocer, you fix the toaster;
You kiss the host goodbye.
Then you break a window, burn the souffle,
Scream the lullaby.

Refrain

And I believe in love.
But what else can I do?
I'm so in love with you.

I know nothing stays the same,
But if you're willing to play the game,
It will be coming around again.

Come On Eileen

Words and Music by Kevin Rowland, James Patterson and Kevin Adams

recorded by Dexys Midnight Runners

Come on Eileen.
Poor old Johnny Ray sounded sad upon the radio;
He moved a million hearts in mono.
Our mothers used to sing along; who'd blame them?

You're grown. (You're grown up.)
So grown. (So grown up.)
Now I must say more than ever.
Come on Eileen.
Too ra, loo ra, roo re loo rye aye.
And we can sing just like our fathers.

Come on Eileen,
Oh, I swear well he means at this moment.
You mean ev'rything.
With you in that dress my thoughts I confess
Verge on dirty ah, come on Eileen.

Come on Eileen.
These people 'round here
Wear beaten down eyes sunk in smoke dried faces,
Resigned to what their fate is,
But not us. No not us.
We are far too young and clever.
Remember too ra, loo ra, roo ra, loo rye aye.
Eileen, I'll hum this tune forever.

Come on Eileen,
Oh, I swear well he means,
Aah come on let's take off ev'ry thing,
That pretty red dress. Eileen, tell him less.
Aah come on let's ah, come on Eileen.

Come on Eileen.
Too loo rye aye come on
Eileen, too loo rye, aye, too ra.
Too ra, too loo ra.
Oh, Eileen.

Come on Eileen,
Oh, I swear well he means at this moment.
You mean ev'rything.
With you in that dress my thoughts I confess
Verge on dirty ah, come on Eileen.

Crazy Little Thing Called Love

Words and Music by Freddie Mercury

recorded by Queen

Verse 1:
This thing called love,
I just can't handle it.
This thing called love,
I must get 'round to it,
I ain't ready.
Crazy little thing called love.

Verse 2:
A-this thing (This thing)
Called love, (Called love)
It cries (Like a baby) in a cradle all night.
It swings, (Oo) it jives, (Oo)
Shakes all over like a jelly fish,
I kinda like it.
Crazy little thing called love.

There goes my baby, she knows how to rock 'n' roll.
She drives me crazy, she gives me hot 'n' cold fever,
She leaves me in a cool, cool sweat.

Verse 3:
I've gotta be cool, relax,
Get hip, get on my tracks,
Take a backseat, hitchhike,
Take a long ride on my motor bike until I'm ready.
Crazy little thing called love.

Repeat Verse 3

Repeat Verse 1

Repeat and Fade:
Crazy little thing called love.

Cuts Like a Knife

Words and Music by Bryan Adams and Jim Vallance

recorded by Bryan Adams

Drivin' home this evenin'
I coulda sworn we had it all worked out.
You had this boy believin'
Way beyond the shadow of a doubt.

Well, I heard it on the street,
I heard you might have found somebody new.
Well, who is he, baby?
Who is he and tell me what he means to you?

I took it all for granted,
But how was I to know that you'd be letting go?
Now it cuts like knife, but it feels so right.
Oh, it cuts like a knife, but it feels so right.

There's times I've been mistaken,
There's times I thought I've been misunderstood.
So wait a minute darlin',
Can't you see we did the best we could?

This wouldn't be the first time
That things have gone astray. Now you've thrown it all away.
Now it cuts like knife, but it feels so right.
Oh, it cuts like a knife, but it feels so right.

Oh, and it cuts like a knife.
And it feels so right, baby.
Oh, and it cuts like a knife.

I took it all for granted,
But how was I to know that you'd be letting go?
Now it cuts like knife, but it feels so right.
And it cuts like a knife, but it feels so right.

Repeat and fade:
Na na na na na na na na na.

Didn't We Almost Have it All

Words and Music by Will Jennings and Michael Masser

recorded by Whitney Houston

Remember when we held on in the rain,
The nights we almost lost it;
Once again we can take the night into tomorrow
Living on feelings.
Touching you, I feel it all again.

Refrain:
Didn't we almost have it all,
When love was all we had worth giving?
The ride with you was worth the fall, my friend;
Loving you makes life worth living.

Didn't we almost have it all,
The nights we held on till the morning?
You know you'll never love that way again;
Didn't we almost have it all?

The way you used to touch me felt so fine;
We kept our hearts together;
Down the line, a moment in the soul can last forever,
Comfort and keep us.
Help me bring the feeling back again.

Refrain

Didn't we almost have it all,
The nights we held on till the morning?
You know you'll never love that way again;
Didn't we almost have it all?

Didn't we have the best of times,
When love was young and new?
Couldn't we reach inside and find
The world of me and you?
We'll never lose it again,
'Cause once you know what love is,
You never let it end.

Didn't we almost have it all,
When love was all we had worth giving?
The ride with you was worth the fall, my friend;
Loving you makes life worth living.

Didn't we almost have it all,
The nights we held on till the morning?
You know you'll never love that way again;
Didn't we almost have it all?
Didn't we almost have it all?

Don't Do Me Like That

Words and Music by Tom Petty

recorded by Tom Petty and The Heartbreakers

I was talkin' with a friend of mine,
Said a woman had hurt his pride.
Told him that she loved him so and
Turned around and let him go.
Then he said, "You better watch your step,
Or you're gonna get hurt yourself.
Someone's gonna tell you lies,
Cut you down to size."

Refrain 1:
Don't do me like that.
Don't do me like that.
What if I loved you, baby?
Don't do me like that.
Don't do me like that.
Don't do me like that.
Someday I might need you, baby.
Don't do me like that.

Listen, honey, can you see?
Baby, it would bury me
If you were in the public eye
Givin' someone else a try.
And you know you better watch your step
Or you're gonna get hurt yourself.
Someone's gonna tell you lies,
Cut you down to size.

Refrain 2:
Don't do me like that.
Don't do me like that.
What if I loved you, baby?
Don't, don't, don't, don't.
Don't do me like that.
Don't do me like that.
Someday I might need you, baby.
Don't do me like that.

'Cause somewhere deep down inside,
someone is sayin', "Love doesn't last that long."
I've had this feelin' inside night out and day in,
And baby, I can't take it no more.

Repeat Verse 2 and Refrain 2

Don't Fall in Love with a Dreamer

Words and Music by Kim Carnes and Dave Ellingson

recorded by Kenny Rogers with Kim Carnes

Just look at you sittin' there,
You never looked better than tonight.
And it'd be so easy to tell you I'd stay,
Like I've done so many times.
I was so sure this would be the night,
You'd close the door and wanna stay with me.
And it's be so easy to tell you I'd stay,
Like I've done so many times.
Don't fall in love with a dreamer,
'Cause he'll always take you in;
Just when you think you've really changed him,
He'll leave you again.

Don't fall in love with a dreamer,
'Cause he'll break you every time;
So, put out the light and just hold on,
Before we say goodbye.
Now it's morning and the phone rings,
And ya say you've gotta get your things together.
You just gotta leave before you change your mind.
And if you knew what I was thinkin', girl,
I'd turn around, if you'd ask me one more time.

Don't fall in love with a dreamer,
'Cause he'll always take you in.
Just when you think you've really changed him,
He'll leave you again.

Don't fall in love with a dreamer,
'Cause he'll break you every time;
So put out the light and just hold on,
Before we say goodbye,
Before we say goodbye, goodbye.

Don't Know Much

Words and Music by Barry Mann, Cynthia Weil and Tom Snow

recorded by Aaron Neville and Linda Ronstadt

Look at this face,
I know the years are showing.
Look at this life,
I still don't know where it's going.

Refrain:
I don't know much,
But I know I love you,
And that may be
All I need to know.

Look at these eyes,
They've never seen what matters.
Look at these dreams,
So beaten and so battered.

Refrain

So many questions
Still left unanswered.
So much I've never broken through.
And when I feel you near me
Sometimes I see so clearly
The only truth I've ever known is me and you.

Look at this man,
So blessed with inspiration.
Look at this soul,
Still searching for salvation.

Refrain Twice

And that may be all there is to know.

Don't You (Forget About Me)

Words and Music by Keith Forsey and Steve Schiff

from the Universal Picture *The Breakfast Club*
recorded by Simple Minds

Won't you come see about me?
I'll be alone dancing. You know it baby.
Tell me your troubles and doubts,
Givin' everything, inside and out.

Love's strange, so real in the dark.
Think of the tender things that we were working on.
Slow change may pull us apart
When the light gets into your heart, baby.

Don't you forget about me.
Don't, don't, don't, don't.
Don't you forget about me.

Will you stand above me,
Look my way, never love me?
Rain keeps falling, rain keeps falling
Down, down, down.

Would you recognize me,
Call my name or walk on by?
Rain keeps falling, rain keeps falling
Down, down, down.

Don't you try and pretend.
It's my feeling we'll win in the end.
I won't harm you or touch your defenses,
Vanity, insecurity.

Don't you forget about me.
I'll be alone dancing. You know it, baby.
Goin' to take you apart.
I'll put us back together at heart, baby.

Don't you forget about me.
Don't, don't, don't, don't.
Don't you forget about me.

But you walk on by.
Will you call my name as you walk on by?
Will you call my name when you walk away,
Or will you walk away?
Will you walk on by?
Come on and call my name.
Will you call my name?

Repeat and Fade:
I say ooh la, la, la, la, la, la, la, la,
La, la, la, la, la, la, la, la, la.

Don't You Want Me

Words and Music by Phil Oakey, Adrian Wright and Jo Callis

recorded by The Human League

You were working as a waitress in a cocktail bar
When I met you.
I picked you out, I shook you up and turned you around,
Turned you into someone new.

Now five years later on you've got the world at your feet.
Success has been so easy for you.
But don't forget it's me who put you where you are now,
And I can put you back there too.

Refrain:
Don't, don't you want me?
You know I can't believe it when I hear that you won't see me.
Don't, don't you want me?
You know I don't believe you when you say that you don't need me.
It's much too late to find when you think you've changed your mind.
You'd better change it back or we will both be sorry.
Don't you want me, baby? Don't you want me, oh?
Don't you want me, baby? Don't you want me, oh?

I was working as a waitress in a cocktail bar,
That much is true.
But even then I knew I'd find a much better place
Either with or without you.

The five years we have had have been such good times,
I still love you.
But now I think it's time I live my life on my own.
I guess it's just what I must do.

Refrain

Repeat and Fade:
Don't you want me, baby?
Don't you want me, oh?

Dreamer

Words and Music by Rick Davies and Roger Hodgson

recorded by Supertramp

Dreamer, you know you are a dreamer.
Well, can you put your hands in your head, oh no.
I said dreamer, you're nothing but a dreamer,
Well, can you put your hands in your head, oh no.

I said far out, what a day, a year, a life it is.
You know, well, you know you had it coming to you.
Now there's not a lot I can do.
Dreamer, you stupid little dreamer,
So now you put your head in your hands, oh no.

I said far out, what a day, a year, a life it is.
You know, well, you know you had it coming to you.
Now there's not a lot I can do.
Work it out someday.

If I could see something (you can see anything you want, boy),
If I could be someone (you can be anyone, celebrate, boy),
Well, if I could do something (you can do something),
If I could do anything (can you do something out of this world).

We'll take a dream on a Sunday.
We'll take a life, take a holiday.
Take a lie, take a dreamer.
(Dream) dream (dream) dream
(Dream) dream (dream) dream along.

(Dreamer) Come on and dream and dream along.
Come on and dream and dream along (come along).
Come on and dream and dream along.
Come on and dream and dream along.

Dreamer, you know you are a dreamer.
Well, can you put your hands in your head, oh no.
I said dreamer, you're nothing but a dreamer,
Well, can you put your hands in your head, oh no. Oh no.

Easy Lover

Words and Music by Phil Collins, Philip Bailey and Nathan East

recorded by Philip Bailey with Phil Collins

Easy lover, she'll get a hold on you, believe it.
Like no other. Before you know it, you'll be on your knees.
She's an easy lover. She'll take your heart, but you won't feel it.
She's like no other, and I'm just tryin' to make you see.

She's the kind of girl you dream of, dream of keeping hold of.
Better forget it. You'll never get it.
She will play around and leave you, leave you and deceive you.
Better forget it. Oh, you'll regret it.
No, you'll never change her, so leave her, leave her.
Get out quick 'cause seeing is believing.
It's the only way you'll ever know.

She's an easy lover, she'll get a hold on you, believe it.
Like no other. Before you know it, you'll be on your knees.
She's an easy lover. She'll take your heart, but you won't feel it.
She's like no other, and I'm just tryin' to make you see.

You're the one that wants to hold her, hold her and control her.
Better forget it. You'll never get it.
'Cause she'll say that there's no other till she finds another.
Better forget it. Oh, you'll regret it.
And don't try to change her. Just leave her, leave her.
You're not the only one, and seeing is believing.
It's the only way you'll ever know.

She's an easy lover, she'll get a hold on you, believe it.
Like no other. Before you know it, you'll be on your knees.
She's an easy lover. She'll take your heart, but you won't feel it.
She's like no other, and I'm just tryin' to make you see.
Try to make you see. She's an easy lover.

Ebony and Ivory

Words and Music by Paul McCartney

recorded by Paul McCartney with Stevie Wonder

Refrain:
Ebony and ivory
Live together in perfect harmony,
Side by side on my piano keyboard,
Oh Lord, why don't we?

We all know that people are the same wherever you go.
There is good and bad in everyone,
We learn to live,
We learn to give each other what we need to survive,
Together alive.

Refrain

Ebony and ivory
Living together in perfect harmony.

867-5309/Jenny

Words and Music by Alex Call and James Keller

recorded by Tommy Tutone

Jenny, Jenny, who can I turn to.
You give me something I can hold onto.
I know you'll think I'm like the others before
Who saw your name and number on the wall.

Refrain:
Jenny, I've got your number,
I need to make you mine.
Jenny, don't change your number.
867-5309. 867-5309.
867-5309. 867-5309.

Jenny, Jenny, you're the girl for me.
You don't know me, but you make me so happy.
I tried to call you before, but I lost my nerve.
I tried my imagination, but I was disturbed.

Refrain

I got it (I got it), I got it,
I got your number on the wall.
I got it (I got it), I got it,
For a good time, for a good time call.

Refrain

Jenny, Jenny, who can I turn to.
867-5309.
For the price of a dime, I can always turn to you.
867-5309.
867-5309.

Endless Love

Words and Music by Lionel Richie

from the film *Endless Love*
recorded by Diana Ross & Lionel Richie

My love,
There's only you in my life,
The only thing that's right.
My first love,
You're every breath that I take,
You're every step I make.
And I,
I want to share all my love with you,
No one else
Will do.
And your eyes,
They tell me how much you care.
Oh yes,
You will always be
My endless love.

Two hearts,
Two hearts that beat as one,
Our lives have just begun.
Forever
I hold you close in my arms
I can't resist your charms.
And love,
I'd be a fool for you.
I'm sure you know
I don't mind,
'Cause you
You mean the world to me.
Oh I know
I found in you
My endless love.

Eternal Flame

Words and Music by Billy Steinberg, Tom Kelly and Susanna Hoffs

recorded by Bangles

Close your eyes
Give me your hand, darling.
Do you feel my heart beating?
Do you understand?
Do you feel the same?
Am I only dreaming?
Is this burning an eternal flame?

I believe it's meant to be, darling.
I watch you when you are sleeping.
You are sleeping.
You belong to me.
Do you feel the same?
Am I only dreaming?
Is the burning an eternal flame?

Refrain:
Say my name,
Sun shines through the rain,
A whole life so lonely,
And then come and ease the pain.
I don't wanna lose this feeling, oh.

Repeat Refrain

Verse 1 Twice

Faithfully

Words and Music by Jonathan Cain

recorded by Journey

Highway, run into the midnight sun.
Wheels go 'round and 'round; you're on my mind.
Restless hearts sleep alone tonight,
Sendin' all my love along the wire.
They say that the road ain't no place to start a family.
Right down the line it's been you and me.
And lovin' a music ain't always what it's supposed to be.
Oh girl, you stand by me. I'm forever yours, faithfully.

Circus life under the big top world;
We all need the clowns to make us smile.
Through space and time always another show.
Wondering where I am; lost without you.
And being apart ain't easy on this love affair;
Two strangers learn to fall in love again.
I get the joy of rediscovering you.
Oh girl, you stand by me. I'm forever yours, faithfully.

Even the Nights Are Better

Words and Music by J. L. Wallace, Terry Skinner and Ken Bell

recorded by Air Supply

I, I was the lonely one,
Wondering what went wrong,
Why love had gone and left me lonely.
I, I was so confused.
Feelin' like I just been used,
Then you came to me and my loneliness left me.

I used to think I was tied to a heartache,
That was the heartbreak, but now that I found you:

Refrain:
Even the nights are better,
Now that we're here together;
Even the nights are better since I found you.
Oh, even the days are brighter
When someone you love's beside ya;
Even the nights are better since I found you.

You, you know just what to do,
'Cause you have been lonely, too,
And you showed me how to ease the pain.
And you did more than end a broken heart,
'Cause now you've made a fire start,
And I, I can see that you feel the same way.

I never dreamed there'd be someone to hold me,
Until you told me, and now that I found you:

Refrain

I never dreamed there'd be someone to hold me
Until you told me, and now that I found you:

Refrain

Every Breath You Take

Music and Lyrics by Sting

recorded by The Police

Every breath you take,
Every move you make,
Every bond you break,
Every step you take,
I'll be watching you.

Every single day,
Every word you say,
Every game you play,
Every night you stay,
I'll be watching you.

Refrain:
Oh, can't you see
You belong to me.
How my poor heart aches
With every step you take.

Every move you make
Every vow you break,
Every smile you fake
Every claim you stake.
I'll be watching you.

Since you've been gone I been lost without a trace,
I dream at night I can only see your face.
I look around but it's you I can't replace,
I feel so cold and I long for your embrace.
I keep crying baby, baby please.

Refrain

Every move you make
Every step you take,
I'll be watching you.
I'll be watching you.

Every Rose Has Its Thorn

Words and Music by Bobby Dall, Brett Michaels,
  Bruce Johannesson and Rikki Rocket

recorded by Poison

We both lie silently still in the dead of the night.
Although we both lie close together, we feel miles apart inside.
Was it something I said or something I did?
Did my words not come out right?
Though I tried not to hurt you, though I tried.
But I guess that's why they say,

Refrain:
Every rose has its thorn,
Just like every night has its dawn.
Just like every cowboy sings his sad, sad song,
Every rose has its thorn.

I listen to our favorite song playing on the radio,
Hear the D.J. say love's a game of easy come and easy go.
But I wonder does he know, has ever felt like this?
And I know that you'd be here right now
If I could've let you know somehow.
I guess

Refrain

Though it's been awhile now I can still feel so much pain.
Like the knife that cuts you, the wound heals,
But the scar, that scar remains.
I know I could have saved our love that night if I'd known what to say.
Instead of making love we both made our separate ways.
Now I hear you've found somebody new and that I never meant that
   much to you.
To hear that tears me up inside
And to see you cuts me like a knife.
I guess

Refrain

Everybody Have Fun Tonight

Words and Music by Wang Chung and Peter Wolf

recorded by Wang Chung

I'd drive a million miles
To be with you tonight.
So if you're feeling low,
Turn up your radio.

The words we use are strong,
They make reality.
But now the music's on,
Oh, baby, dance with me.

Pick it up. Move down. Pick it up.
Move it down to the ground.
Pick it up. Move down. Pick it up.
Don't hang it on the borderline.

Ev'rybody have fun tonight.
Ev'rybody have fun to night.
Ev'rybody Wang Chung tonight.
Ev'rybody have fun tonight.
Ev'rybody Wang Chung tonight.
Ev'rybody have fun.

Deep in the world tonight
I hope it's safe and sound.
I'll hold you so close,
Just let yourself go down.

Pick it up. Move down. Pick it up.
Move it down to the ground.
Pick it up. Move down. Pick it up.
And gather what's inside of you.

Ev'rybody have fun tonight.
Ev'rybody have fun to night.
Ev'rybody Wang Chung tonight.
Ev'rybody have fun tonight.
Ev'rybody Wang Chung tonight.
Ev'rybody have fun tonight.
Ev'rybody have fun.

Oh, the age of oblivion
And all the world is Babylon.
And all the lovers and ev'ryone,
A ship of fools sailing on.

Ev'rybody, ev'rybody have fun tonight.
Ev'rybody, ev'rybody have fun tonight.
Across the nation, around the world,
Ev'rybody have fun tonight.
A celebration, so spread the word.

Repeat Three Times:
Ev'rybody have fun tonight.
Ev'rybody have fun to night.
Ev'rybody Wang Chung tonight.
Ev'rybody have fun tonight.
Ev'rybody Wang Chung tonight.
Ev'rybody have fun tonight.

Ev'rybody have fun.

Repeat and Fade:
Ev'rybody. Ev'ryone.

Everybody Wants to Rule the World

Words and Music by Ian Stanley, Roland Orzabal and Chris Hughes

recorded by Tears for Fears

Welcome to your life;
There's no turning back.
Even while we sleep we will find you
Acting on your best behavior;
Turn your back on mother nature.
Everybody wants to rule the world.

There's a room where the light won't find you
Holding hands while the walls come tumbling down.
When they do, I'll be right behind you.

So glad we've almost made it.
So sad they had to fade it.
Everybody wants to rule the world.

It's my own design,
It's my own remorse,
Help me to decide.
Help me make the most of freedom and of pleasure,
Nothing ever lasts forever.
Everybody wants to rule the world.

I can't stand this indecision
Married with a lack of vision.
Everybody wants to rule the world.

Say that you'll never, never, never need it.
One headline, why believe it?
Everybody wants to rule the world.

All for freedom and for pleasure,
Nothing ever lasts forever.
Everybody wants to rule the world.

Fast Car

Words and Music by Tracy Chapman

recorded by Tracy Chapman

You got a fast car.
I want a ticket to anywhere.
Maybe we make a deal.
Maybe together we can get somewhere.
Anyplace is better.
Starting from zero got nothing to lose.
Maybe we'll make something.
Me, myself I've got nothing to prove.

You got a fast car.
I got a plan to get us out of here.
Been working at the convenience store.
Managed to save just a little bit of money.
Won't have to drive too far,
Just cross the border and into the city.
You and I can both get jobs and
Finally see what it means to be living.

See my old man's problem.
He live with the bottle, that's the way it is.
He says his body's too old for working.
His body's too young to look like his.
My mama went off and left him.
She wanted more from life than he could give.
I said somebody's got to take care of him.
So I quit school and that's what I did.

You got a fast car.
Is it fast enough so we could fly away?
We gotta make a decision,
Leave tonight or live and die this way.

Refrain:
I remember when we were driving,
Driving in your car,
Speed so fast I felt like I was drunk,
City lights lay out before us
And your arms felt nice wrapped 'round my shoulder,
And I had a feeling that I belonged.
I had a feeling I could be someone,
Be someone, be someone.

You got a fast car.
We go cruising, entertain ourselves.
You still ain't got a job
And I work in the market as a check-out girl.
I know things will get better.
You'll find work and I'll get promoted.
We'll move out of the shelter,
Buy a big house and live in the suburbs.

Refrain

You got a fast car.
I got a job that pays all our bills.
You stay out drinking late at the bar,
See more of your friends than you do of your kids.
I'd always hoped for better,
Thought maybe together you and me'd find it.
I got no plans, I ain't going nowhere;
So take your fast car and keep on driving.

Refrain

You got a fast car.
Is it fast enough so you could fly away?
You gotta make a decision,
Leave tonight or live and die this way.

The Flame

Words and Music by Bob Mitchell and Nick Graham

recorded by Cheap Trick

Another night slowly closes in
And it feels so lonely.
Touching heat, freezing on my skin,
I pretend you still hold me.
I'm goin' crazy, I'm losin' sleep.
I'm in too far, I'm in way too deep over you.
I can't believe you're gone.

Refrain:
You were the first, you'll be the last.
Wherever you go, I'll be with you.
Whatever you want, I'll give it to you.
Whenever you need someone to lay your heart and head upon,
Remember: after the fire, after all the rain,
I will be the flame. I will be the flame.

Watchin' shadows move across the wall,
I feel so frightened.
I wanna run to you, I wanna call,
But I've been hit by lightning.
Just can't stand up for fallin' apart,
Can't see through this veil cross my heart, over you.
You'll always be the one.

Refrain

I'm goin' crazy, I'm losin' sleep.
I'm in too far, I'm in way too deep over you.
You'll always be the one.

Refrain

Repeat and Fade:
I will be the flame.
Whatever you want, I'll give it to you.
Wherever you go, I'll be with you.

Footloose

Words by Dean Pitchford and Kenny Loggins
Music by Kenny Loggins

Theme from the Paramount Picture *Footloose*
recorded by Kenny Loggins

I been workin' so hard. I'm punchin' my card.
Eight hours, for what? Oh, tell me what I got.
I've got this feelin' that time's just holdin' me down.
I'll hit the ceiling, or else I'll tear up this town.

Tonight I gotta cut loose, footloose;
Kick off your Sunday shoes.
Please, Louise, pull me off of my knees.
Jack, get back; come on before we crack.
Lose your blues, ev'rybody cut footloose.

You're playin' so cool, obeying ev'ry rule.
Dig way down in your heart, you're burnin', yearnin' for some,
Somebody to tell you that life ain't passin' you by.
I'm tryin' to tell you it will if you don't even fly.

You can fly if you'd only cut loose, footloose;
Kick off your Sunday shoes.
Ooh-ee, Marie, shake it, shake it for me.
Whoa, Milo, come on, come on let's go.
Lose your blues, ev'rybody cut footloose.

First, you've got to turn me around,
Second, and put your feet on the ground.
Third, now, take a hold of your soul.

I'm turnin' it loose, footloose;
Kick off your Sunday shoes.
Please, Louise, pull me off of my knees.
Jack, get back; come on before we crack.

Lose your blues, ev'rybody cut, ev'rybody cut,
Ev'rybody cut, ev'rybody cut,
Spoken: Ev'rybody cut, ev'rybody cut, ev'rybody,
Sung: Ev'rybody cut footloose.

Forever Young

Words and Music by Rod Stewart, Jim Cregan, Kevin Savigar and Bob Dylan

recorded by Rod Stewart

May the good Lord be with you
Down every road you roam.
And may sunshine and happiness
Surround you when you're far from home.

And may you grow to be proud,
Dignified and true.
And do unto others
As you'd have done to you.
Be courageous and be brave.
And in my heart you'll always stay

Refrain:
Forever young,
Forever young,
Forever young,
Forever young.

May good fortune be with you,
May your guiding light be strong,
Build a stairway to heaven
With a prince or a vagabond.
And may you never love in vain.
And in my heart you will remain

Refrain

Forever young,
Forever young.

And when you finally fly away,
I'll be hoping that I served you well.
For all the wisdom of a lifetime,
No one can ever tell.
But whatever road you choose,
I'm right behind you, win or lose.

Refrain Twice

Forever Your Girl

Words and Music by Oliver Leiber

recorded by Paula Abdul

Hey baby, just remember
I'm forever your girl.
Baby, forever, and ever and ever,
Spoken: You know I am.
Sung: Baby, pick your head up, (head up,)
Come on and look me in the face,
'Cause I can tell that something
Is bringin' you down. (Why are you down?)
Is it the rumor that another boy
Wants to take your place? (I hear he's after your heart.)
Have you been hearin' the stories?
They're goin' around. (All of my friends are talkin'.)
Baby, just remember I gave you my heart,
Ain't no one gonna tear us apart.
He can promise the moon and the stars above,
Even if he promised me the world.

Refrain:
Just remember I'm forever your girl.
He could promise the world,
Just remember, I'm forever your girl.

Hey listen to me, your love is all I need.
You should know that I don't need nothin'
That money can buy.
So if a boy were to come along
And try to make me leave you,
(Girl, I'd be out of my mind,)
There'd be no reason to worry,
I'm tellin' you why.
(I need to hear that you really love me.)
Baby, don't you know that I love you.
And I'd never put nobody above you.
He could promise the moon and the stars above,
Even if he promised me the world.

Just remember I'm forever your girl.
He could promise the world,
Just remember, I'm forever your girl.
I'm forever your baby.
Just remember I'm forever your girl.
He could promise the world,
Just remember, I'm forever your girl.

When the mountains crumble into the sea,
That's the day someone will come between you and me.
Baby just remember I gave you my heart,
Ain't no one gonna tear us apart.
Baby, he could promise me diamonds,
Even if he promised me pearls;
Honey, you know I ain't lyin',
Listen as I tell it to the world.

Just remember I'm forever your girl.
He could promise the world,
Just remember, I'm forever your girl.

Repeat and Fade:
I'm forever your girl.

Free Fallin'

Words and Music by Tom Petty and Jeff Lynne

recorded by Tom Petty

She's a good girl; loves her mama.
Loves Jesus, and America too.
She's a good girl, crazy 'bout Elvis;
Loves horses and her boyfriend too.

It's a long day livin' in Reseda.
There's a freeway runnin' through the yard.
And I'm a bad boy 'cause I don't even miss her.
I'm a bad boy for breakin' her heart.

And I'm free, free fallin'
Yeah, I'm free, free fallin'.

All the vampires walkin' through the valley
Move west down Ventura Boulevard.
And all the bad boys are standing in the shadows.
And the good girls are home with broken hearts.

And I'm free, free fallin'
Yeah, I'm free, free fallin'.

Wanna glide down over Mulholland.
I wanna write her name in the sky.
I wanna free fall out into nothin'.
Gonna leave this world for awhile.

And I'm free, free fallin'
Yeah, I'm free, free fallin'.
And I'm free, free fallin'.
Yeah, I'm free, free fallin'.

Girls Just Want to Have Fun

Words and Music by Robert Hazard

recorded by Cyndi Lauper

I come home in the morning light.
My mother ways, "When you gonna live your life right?"
Oh, Mother dear, we're not the fortunate ones.
And girls, they just want to have fun.
Oh, girls just want to have fun.

The phone rings in the middle of the night.
My father yells, "What you gonna do with your life?"
Oh, Daddy dear, you know you're still number one.
But girls just want to have…
That's all they really want:
Some fun.
When the working day is done,
Oh, girls, they want to have fu-un.
Oh, girls just want to have fun.

Some boys take a beautiful girl
And hide her away from the rest of the world.
I want to be the one to walk in the sun.
Oh, girls just want to have…
That's all they really want:
Some fun.
When the working day is done,
Oh, girls, they want to have fu-un.
Oh, girls just want to have fun.

They just wanna,
They just wanna.
They just wanna,
Girls, girls just want to have fu-un.

Get Outta My Dreams, Get into My Car

Words and Music by Billy Ocean and Robert John Lange

recorded by Billy Ocean

Who's that lady coming down the road?
Who's that lady?
Who's that woman walking through my door?
What's the score?

I'll be the sun shining on you.
Hey Cinderella, step in your shoe.
I'll be your nonstop lover, get it while you can.
Your nonstop miracle, I'm your man.

Get outta my dreams, get into my car!
Get outta my dreams, get in the backseat baby.
Get into my car. (Beep, beep, yeah.)
Get outta my mind. Get into my life.
Oh, I said, "Hey you, get into my car."

Lady driver let me take your wheel.
Smooth operator
Touch my bumper, hey let's make a deal,
Make it real.
Like a road runner coming after you,
Just like a hero outta the blue.
I'll be your nonstop lover, get it while you can.
Your nonstop miracle, I'm your man.

Get outta my dreams, get into my car!
Get outta my dreams. Get in the backseat baby.
Get into my car. (Beep, beep, yeah.)
Get outta my mind. Get into my life.
Oh, I said hey you, get into my car.
Oh, baby, let's go!

I said open the door, get in the back,
Foot on the floor, get on the track.
Yeah, yeah, yeah, yeah. Let's go!
Oh, babe. Oo. Yeah.

I'll be the sun shining on you.
Hey Cinderella, step in your shoe.
I'll be your nonstop lover, get it while you can.
Your nonstop miracle, I'm your man.

Get outta my dreams, Get into my car!
Get outta my dreams. Get in the backseat baby.
Get into my car. (Beep, beep, yeah.)
Get outta my mind. Get into my life.
Oh, I said hey you, get into my, hey you,
Get into my, hey you, get into my car!

Girl You Know It's True

Words and Music by Bill Pettaway, Kevin Liles, Rodney Holloman,
  Sean Spencer and Kayode Adeyemo

recorded by Milli Vanilli

Rap:

I'm in love with you girl, 'cause you're on my mind,
You're the one I think about most every time.
And when you pack a smile in everything you do,
Don't you understand, girl, this love is true?
You're soft, succulent, so sweet and thin.
That's kind of like a vision upon your skin.
It lightens up my day, and that's oh, so true.
Together we're one, separated we're two.
To make you all mine, all mine is my desire
'Cause you contain a quality, you, that I admire.
You're pretty, plain and simple, you rule my world,
So try to understand.
I'm in love, girl, I'm so in love, girl.
I'm just in love, girl, and this is true.

Refrain, sung:

Girl, you know it's true. Ooh, ooh, ooh, I love you.
Yes, you know it's true. Ooh, ooh, ooh, I love you.
Girl you know it's true. My love is for you.
Girl you know it's true. My love is for you.

Rap:

This is some sort of thing, girl, I can't explain.
My emotions start up when I hear your name.
Maybe your sweet, sweet voice would ring in my ear,
Then delay my system when you are near.
Come with your positive emotion, love, making, enjoying.
That's for me to bust. It's like a girl and a boy.
These feelings I get, I often wonder why,
So I thought I might discuss this, girl, just you and I.
Now what you're wearing, I don't care, as I've said before.
No reason that I like you girl, just for what you are.
If I said I'd think about it, you rule my world, so try to understand.
I'm in love, girl, I'm so in love, girl.
I'm just in love, girl, and this is true.

Refrain

Girl, you know it's true. Ooh, ooh, ooh, I love you.
Yes, you know it's true. Ooh, ooh, ooh, I love you.

Give Me the Night

Words and Music by Rod Temperton

recorded by George Benson

Whenever dark is fallin',
You know the spirit of the party starts to come alive.
Until the day is dawnin',
You can throw out all the blues and hit the city lights,

Refrain:
'Cause there's music in the air,
And lots of lovin' everywhere,
So give me the night.
Give me the night.

You need the evenin' action,
A place to dine, a glass of wine, a little romance.
It's a chain reaction,
We'll see the people of the world comin' out to dance.

Refrain Twice

And if we stay together,
We'll feel the rhythm of the evening takin' us up high.
Never mind the weather,
We'll be dancin' in the street until the morning light.

Refrain

Gloria

Original Words and Music by Giancarlo Bigazzi and Umberto Tozzi
English Lyrics by Trevor Veitch

recorded by Laura Brannigan

Gloria, you're always on the run now.
Runnin' after somebody, you gotta get him somehow.
I think you've gotta slow down before you stop growing.
I think you're headed for a breakdown.

You're careful not to show it.
You really don't remember.
Was it something that he said,
Or the voices in your head calling Gloria?

Gloria, don't you think you're falling?
If everybody wants you, why isn't anybody calling?
You don't have to answer,
Leave them hanging on the love line calling Gloria.

Gloria, I think they've got your number,
I think they've got the alias that you've been living under.
But you really don't remember. Was it something that they said
Or the voices in your head calling Gloria?

Repeat and Fade:
Gloria, Gloria.

Glory of Love

Words and Music by David Foster, Peter Cetera and Diane Nini

Theme from *Karate Kid Part II*
recorded by Peter Cetera

Tonight it's very clear,
As we're both standing here,
There's so many things I want to say.
I will always love you,
I will never leave you alone.
Sometimes I just forget,
Say things I might regret,
It breaks my heart to see you crying.
I don't want to lose you,
I could never make it alone.

Refrain:
I am a man
Who would fight for your honor,
I'll be the hero you're dreaming of.
We'll live forever,
Knowing together,
That we did it all
For the glory of love.

You keep me standing tall,
You help me through it all,
I'm always strong
When you're beside me.
I have always needed you,
I could never make it alone.

Refrain

Just like the a knight in shining armor,
From a long time ago,
Just in time I will save the day,
Take you to my castle far away.

I am the man
Who will fight for your honor,
I'll be the hero that you're dreaming of.
We're gonna live forever,
Knowing together,
That we did it all
For the glory of love.

We'll live forever,
Knowing together,
That we did it all
For the glory of love.
We did it all for love.

Got My Mind Set on You

Words and Music by Rudy Clark

recorded by George Harrison

I got my mind set on you,
I got my mind set on you,
I got my mind set on you,
Got my mind set on you.
But it's gonna take money.
A whole lotta spending money.
It's gonna take plenty of money
To do it right, child.

It's gonna take time,
A whole lotta precious time.
It's gonna take patience and time
To do it,
To do it,
To do it,
To do it,
To do it,
To do it right, child.

I got my mind set on you,
I got my mind set on you,
I got my mind set on you,
I got my mind set on you.
And this time I know it's real
The feeling that I feel.
I know if I put my mind to it,
I know that I really can do it.
I got my mind set on you, set on you.

Heart and Soul

Words and Music by Mike Chapman and Nicky Chinn

recorded by Huey Lewis and The News

Two o'clock this morning
If she should come a calling
I wouldn't dream of turning her away.
And if it got hot and hectic
I know she'd be electric.
I'd let her take her chances with me.
You see, she gets what she wants

'Cause she's heart and soul.
She's hot and cold.
She's got it all.
Hot loving every night.

Well, can't you see her standing there?
See how she looks, see how she cares.
I let her steal the night away from me.
Nine o'clock this morning
She left without a warning.
I let her take advantage of me.
You see, she got what she wanted

'Cause she's heart and soul
She's hot and cold
She's got it all.
Hot loving every night.

Guilty

Words and Music by Barry Gibb, Robin Gibb and Maurice Gibb

recorded by Barbra Streisand & Barry Gibb

Shadows falling, baby,
We stand alone
Out on the street anybody you meet
Got a heartache of their own.
Make it a crime to be lonely or sad.
You got a reason for living,
You battle on
With the love you're livin' on,
You gotta be mine.
We take it away.
It's gotta be night and day,
Just a matter of time.

Refrain:
And we got nothing to be guilty of.
Our love will climb any mountain
Near or far, we are,
And we never let it end.
We are devotion
And we got nothing to be sorry for.
Our love is one in a million.
Eyes can see that we got a highway to the sky.
I don't want to hear your goodbye.

Pulse's racing, darling,
How grand we are.
Little by little we meet in the middle,
There's danger in the dark.
Make it a crime to be out in the cold.
You got a reason for livin',
You battle on
With the love you're buildin' on, you gotta be mine.
We take it away.
It's gotta be night and day,
Just a matter of time.

Refrain

Don't wanna hear your goodbye.
I don't wanna hear your—
And we got nothing,

Refrain

Hard to Say I'm Sorry

Words and Music by Peter Cetera and David Foster

recorded by Chicago

Everybody needs a little time away,
I heard her say,
From each other.
Even lovers need a holiday,
Far away
From each other.
Hold me now.
It's hard for me to say I'm sorry.
I just want you to stay.

After all that we've been through,
I will make it up to you.
I'll promise to.
And after all that's been said and done
You're just the part of me I can't let go.

Couldn't stand to be kept away,
Just for the day,
From your body.
Wouldn't wanna be swept away,
Far away,
From the one that I love.
Hold me now.
It's hard for me to say I'm sorry.
I just want you to know.
Hold me now.
I really want to tell you I'm sorry.
I could never let you go.

After all that we've been through,
I will make it up to you.
I'll promise to.
And after all that's been said and done

You're just the part of me I can't let go.
After all that we've been through,
I will make it up to you.
I'll promise to.
You're gonna be the lucky one.

Heartbreaker

Words and Music by Cliff Wade and Geoff Gill

recorded by Pat Benatar

Your love is like a tidal wave spinnin' over my head,
Drownin' me in your promises better left unsaid.
You're the right kind of sinner to release my inner fantasy,
The invincible winner and you know that you were born to be.

Refrain:
You're a heartbreaker, dream maker, love taker,
Don't you mess around with me!
You're a heartbreaker, dream maker, love taker,
Don't you mess around, no, no, no!

Your love has set my soul on fire, burnin' out of control.
You taught me the ways of desire, now it's taken its toll.
You're the right kind of sinner to release my inner fantasy,
The invincible winner and you know that you were born to be.

Refrain

You're the right kind of sinner to release my inner fantasy,
The invincible winner and you know that you were born to be.

You're a heartbreaker, dream maker, love taker,
Don't you mess around with me!
You're a heartbreaker, dream maker, love taker,
Don't you mess around with me!

You're a heartbreaker, dream maker, love taker,
Don't you mess around with me!
You're a heartbreaker, dream maker, love taker,
Heartbreaker.

Hello

Words and Music by Lionel Richie

recorded by Lionel Richie

I've been alone with you inside my mind.
And in my dreams I've kissed your lips a thousand times.
I sometimes see you pass outside my door.
Hello, is it me you're lookin' for?

I can see it in your eyes, I can see it in your smile.
You're all I've ever wanted and my arms are open wide.
'Cause you know just what to say and you know just what to do
And I want to tell you so much, "I love you."

I long to see the sunlight in your hair.
And tell you time and time again how much I care.
Sometimes I feel my heart will overflow.
Hello, I just got to let you know.

'Cause I wonder where you are, and I wonder what you do.
Are you somewhere feeling lonely or is someone loving you?
Tell me how to win your heart, for I haven't got a clue,
But let me start by saying, "I love you."

Hello, is it me you're looking for?
'Cause I wonder where you are and I wonder what you do.
Are you somewhere feeling lonely or is someone lovin' you?
Tell me how to win your heart, I don't even have a clue.
But let me start by saying, "Ooh, I love you."

Heaven

Words and Music by Bryan Adams and Jim Vallance

recorded by Bryan Adams

Oh, thinkin' about all our younger years.
There was only you and me,
We were young and wild and free.
Now nothin' can take you away from me.
We've been down that road before,
But that's over now, you keep me comin' back for more.

Refrain:
Baby, you're all that I want
When you're lyin' here in my arms.
I'm findin' it hard to believe we're in heaven.
And love is all that I need,
And I found it there in your heart.
It isn't too hard to see we're in heaven.

Oh, once in your life you find someone
Who will turn your world around,
Bring you up when you're feelin' down.
Yeah, nothin' could change what you mean to me.
Oh, there's lots that I could say,
But just hold me now, 'cause our love will light the way.

Refrain

I've been waitin' for so long
For somethin' to arrive,
For love to come along.
Now our dreams are comin' true.
Through the good times and the bad,
Yeah, I'll be standin' there by you.

Refrain

Heaven.
You're all that I want, you're all that I need.

Heaven Is a Place on Earth

Words and Music by Rick Nowels and Ellen Shipley

recorded by Belinda Carlisle

Refrain:
Ooh, baby, do you know what that's worth?
Ooh, heaven is a place on earth.
They say in heaven love comes first.
We'll make heaven a place on earth.
Ooh, heaven is a place on earth.

When the night falls down,
I wait for you and you come around.
And the world's alive with the sound of kids
On the street outside.

When you walk into the room,
You pull me close and we start to move.
And we're spinning with the stars above
And you lift me up in a wave of love.

Refrain

When I feel alone, I reach for you
And you bring me home.
When I'm lost at sea, I hear your voice
And it carries me.

In this world we're just beginning
To understand the miracle of living.
Baby, I was afraid before
But I'm not afraid anymore.

Refrain

In this world we're just beginning
To understand the miracle of living.
Baby, I was afraid before
But I'm not afraid anymore.

Refrain

Repeat and Fade:
Ooh, heaven is a place on earth.

Higher Love

Words and Music by Will Jennings and Steve Winwood

recorded by Steve Winwood

Think about it, there must be higher love,
Down in the heart or hidden in the stars above.
Without it, life is wasted time.
Look inside your heart, I'll look inside mine.

Refrain:
Things look so bad everywhere.
In this whole world what is fair?
We walk blind and we try to see,
Falling behind in what could be.
Bring me a higher love,
Bring me a higher love, whoa.
Bring me a higher love.

Where's that higher love I keep thinking of.

Worlds are turning and we're just hanging on,
Facing our fear and standing out there alone.
A yearning, and it's real to me.
There must be someone who's feeling for me.

Refrain

I could rise above on a higher love.

I will not wait for it.
I'm not too late for it.
Until then, I'll sing my song
To cheer the night along.
Bring it.

I could light the night up with my soul on fire.
I could make the sunshine from pure desire.
Let me feel that love come over me.
Let me feel how strong it could be.

Repeat and Fade:
Bring me a higher love,
Bring me a higher love, whoa.
Bring me a higher love,
Bring me a higher love.

Hit Me with Your Best Shot

Words and Music by Eddie Schwartz

recorded by Pat Benatar

Well, you're a real tough cookie
With a long history
Of breaking little hearts
Like the one in me.
That's O.K.
Let's see how you do it.
Put up your dukes.
Let's get down to it.

Refrain:
Hit me with your best shot.
Why don't you
Hit me with your best shot?
Hit me with your best shot.
Fire away.

You come on with a come on.
You don't fight fair.
But that's O.K.
See if I care.
Knock me down.
It's all in vain.
I'll get right back on
My feet again.

Refrain

Well, you're a real tough cookie
With a long history
Of breaking little hearts
Like the one in me.
Before I put another notch
In my lipstick case,
You better make sure
You put me in my place.

Refrain

Hold Me

Words and Music by Christine McVie and Robbie Patton

recorded by Fleetwood Mac

Can you understand me? Baby, don't you hand me a line.
Although it doesn't matter, you and me got plenty of time.
There's nobody in the future, so baby, let me hand you my love.
Oh, no step for you to dance to, so slip your hand inside of my glove.

Refrain:
Hold me. Hold me.
Hold me. Hold me.

I don't want no damage, but how am I gonna manage you?
Oh, you want a percentage, but I'm the fool payin' the dues.
I'm a just around the corner if you got a minute to spare.
And I'll be waitin' for ya if you ever wanna be there.

Refrain Twice

Hold me. Hold me.

Hold On Loosely

Words and Music by Don Barnes, Jeff Carlisi and James Michael Peterik

recorded by .38 Special

You see it all around you: good lovin' gone bad.
And you believe it's too late when you realize what you had.
And my mind goes back to a girl that I left
Some years ago, who told me:

Just hold on loosely, but don't let go.
If you cling too tightly, you're gonna lose control.
Your baby needs someone to believe in
And a whole lot of space to breathe in.

So damn easy when your feelings are such,
To overprotect her, to love her too much.
And my mind goes back to a girl that I left
Some years ago, who told me:

Just hold on loosely, but don't let go.
If you cling too tightly, you're gonna lose control.
Your baby needs someone to believe in
And a whole lot of space to breathe in.

Don't let her slip away. Sentimental fool.
Don't let your heart get in the way.

Just hold on loosely, but don't let go.
If you cling too tightly, you're gonna lose control.
Your baby needs someone to believe in
And a whole lot of space to breathe in.

Hold Me Now

Words and Music by Tom Bailey, Alannah Currie and Joe Leeway

recorded by Thompson Twins

I have a picture pinned to my wall,
An image of you and of me
And we're laughing with love at it all.
Look at our life now, tattered and torn,
We fuss and we fight and delight
In the tears that we cry until dawn.

Refrain:
Oh, oh hold me now. (In your lovin' arms)
Oh warm my heart, (warm my cold and tired heart)
Stay with me (ooh stay with me)
Let lovin' start, let lovin' start.

You say I'm a dreamer, we're two of a kind,
Both of us searching for some perfect world
We know we'll never find.
So perhaps I should leave here, yeah, yeah, go far away,
But you know that there's nowhere that I'd rather be
Than with you here today.

Refrain

Oh hold me now, oh warm my heart,
Stay with me, let lovin' start,
Let lovin' start, oh.

You asked if I love you, what can I say?
You know that I do and that this
Is just one of those games that we play.
So I'll sing you a new song, please don't cry anymore,
I'll even ask your forgiveness
Though I don't know just what I'm asking it for. Oh, oh.

Refrain

Oh hold me now, oh warm my heart,
Stay with me, let lovin' start,
Let lovin' start, oh.

Holding Back the Years

Words by Mick Hucknall
Music by Mick Hucknall and Neil Moss

recorded by Simply Red

Holding back the years,
Thinking of the fear I've had so long
When somebody hears,
Listen to the fear that's gone.
Strangled by the wishes of pater,
Hoping for the arms of mater,
Get to meet her sooner or later.

Holding back the years,
Chance for me to escape from all I've known.
Holding back the tears,
'Cause nothing here has grown.
I've wasted all my tears,
Wasted all those years.
Nothing had the chance to be good,
Nothing ever could, yeah.

Refrain:
I'll keep holding on,
I'll keep holding on,
I'll keep holding on,
I'll keep holding on.

Well I've wasted all my tears,
Wasted all of those years.
And nothing had a chance to be good,
'Cause nothing ever could.

Refrain

Holding, holding, holding.
That's all I have today.
It's all I have to say.

How Will I Know

Words and Music by George Merrill, Shannon Rubicam and Narada Michael Walden

recorded by Whitney Houston

There's a boy I know, he's the one I dream of.
Looks into my eyes; takes me into the clouds above.

Oh, I lose control; can't seem to get enough.
When I wake from dreamin'; tell me, is it really love?

How will I know?
(Girl, trust your feelings.)
How will I know?
How will I know?
(Love can be deceivin'.)
How will I know?

Refrain:
How will I know if he really loves me?
I say a prayer with every heartbeat.
I fall in love whenever we meet.
I'm askin' you, 'cause you know about these things.
How will I know if he's thinkin' of me?
I try to phone, but I'm too shy.
(Can't speak.)
Falling in love is so bittersweet.
This love is strong.
Why do I feel weak?

Oh, wake me, I'm shakin'; wish I had you near me now.
Said there's no mistakin'; what I feel is really love.

How will I know?
(Girl, trust your feelings.)
How will I know?
How will I know?
(Love can be deceiving.)
How will I know?

Refrain

If he loves me;
If he loves me not.
If he loves me;
If he loves me not.
If he loves me;
If he loves me not. Oh,

Refrain

Human

Words and Music by James Harris III and Terry Lewis

recorded by The Human League

Come on baby, dry your eyes,
Wipe your tears.
Never like to see you cry.
Spoken: Won't you please forgive me?

Sung: I wouldn't ever try to hurt you.
I just needed someone to hold me,
To fill the void while you were gone,
To fill this space of emptiness.

Refrain:
I'm only human,
Of flesh and blood I'm made.
Human, born to make mistakes.

So many nights I longed to hold you.
So many times I looked and saw your face.
Nothing could change the way I feel,
No one else could ever take your place.

Refrain

I am just a man.
Human. Ooh, human.
Spoken: Please forgive me.

Spoken: The tears I cry aren't tears of pain,
They're only to hide my guilt and shame.
I forgive you, now I ask the same of you.
While we were apart I was human too.

Sung: Ooh, Human.
Ooh, Human.

I'm only human,
Of flesh and blood I'm made.
I am just a man.
Human, born to make mistakes.

Repeat and Fade:
Human, ooh human.

Hungry Eyes

Words and Music by Franke Previte and John DeNicola

from the Vestron Motion Picture *Dirty Dancing*
recorded by Eric Carmen

I've been meaning to tell you
I've got this feeling that won't subside.
I look at you and I fantasize you're mine tonight.
Now I've got you in my sights
With these hungry eyes.

One look at you and I can't disguise
I've got hungry eyes.
I feel the magic between you and I.

I want to hold you, so hear me out.
I want to show you what love's all about,
Darling, tonight.
Now I've got you in my sights
With these hungry eyes.

One look at you and I can't disguise
I've got hungry eyes.
I feel the magic between you and I.
I've got hungry eyes.

Now I've got you in my sights
With those hungry eyes.
Now, did I take you by surprise?
I need you to see this love was meant to be.
I've got hungry eyes.

One look at you and I can't disguise
I've got hungry eyes.
I feel the magic between you and I.
I've got hungry eyes.

Now I've got you in my sights
With those hungry eyes.
Now did I take you by surprise?
I need you to see this love was meant to be.

Hurts So Good

Words and Music by John Mellencamp and George Green

recorded by John Cougar

When I was a young boy,
Said, put away those young boy ways.
Now that I'm gettin' older, so much older,
I love all those young boy days.
With a girl like you, with a girl like you,
Lord knows there are things we can do, baby, just me and you.
Come on and make it

Refrain:
Hurt so good.
Come on, baby, make it hurt so good.
Sometimes love don't feel like it should.
You make it hurt so good.

Don't have to be so exciting.
Just try'n' to give myself a little bit of fun, yeah.
You always look so inviting.
You ain't as green as you are young.
Hey, baby, it's you. Come on, girl, now, it's you.
Sink your teeth right through my bones, baby.
Let's see what we can do.
Come on and make it

Refrain

I ain't talkin' no big deals;
I ain't made no plans myself.
I ain't talkin' no high heels.
Maybe we could walk around all day long,
Walk around all day long.

Refrain Twice

It's My Life

Words and Music by Mark David Hollis and Tim Frese-Greene

recorded by Talk Talk

It's funny how I find myself in love with you.
If I could buy my reasoning, I'd pay to lose.
One half won't do.
I've asked myself how much do you commit yourself?
Oh, it's my life. Don't you forget.
It's my life. It never ends.

Funny how I blind myself. I never knew
If I was sometimes played upon, afraid to lose.
I'd tell myself what good do you do, convince myself.
Oh, it's my life. Don't you forget.
It's my life. It never ends.

I've asked myself, how much do you commit yourself?
Oh, it's my life. Don't you forget.
Caught in the crowd. It never ends.
It's my life. Don't you forget.
Caught in the crowd. It never ends.

I Just Called to Say I Love You

Words and Music by Stevie Wonder

recorded by Stevie Wonder

No New Year's Day
To celebrate;
No chocolate-covered candy hearts
To give away.
No first of spring;
No song to sing.
In fact here's just another ordinary day.

No April rain;
No flowers bloom;
No wedding Saturday within
The month of June.
But what it is
Is something true,
Made up of these three words
I must say to you.

Refrain:
I just called to say I love you.
I just called to say how much I care.
I just called to say I love you.
And I mean it from the bottom of my heart.

No summer's high;
No warm July;
No harvest moon to light
One tender August night.
No autumn breeze;
No falling leaves;
Not even time for birds to fly
To southern skies.

No Libra sun;
No Halloween;
No giving thanks to all
The Christmas joy you bring.
But what it is,
Though old so new
To fill your heart like no
Three words could ever do.

Refrain Twice

I Love a Rainy Night

Words and Music by Eddie Rabbitt, Even Stevens and David Malloy

recorded by Eddie Rabbitt

Well, I love a rainy night;
I love a rainy night.
I love to hear the thunder, watch the lightning
When it lights up the sky,
You know it makes me feel good.
Well, I love a rainy night;
It's such a beautiful sight.
I love to feel the rain on my face,
Taste the rain on my lips
In the moonlight shadows.
Showers wash all my cares away;
I wake up to a sunny day.

Refrain:
'Cause I love a rainy night,
Yeah, I love a rainy night.
Well, I love a rainy night.
Well, I love a rainy night.

Well, I love a rainy night;
I love a rainy night.
I love to hear the thunder, watch the lightning
When it lights up the sky,
You know it makes me feel good.
Well, I love a rainy night;
It's such a beautiful sight.
I love to feel the rain on my face,
Taste the rain on my lips
In the moonlight shadows.
Puts a song in this heart of mine;
Puts a smile on my face every time.

Refrain

I Love Rock 'n Roll

Words and Music by Alan Merrill and Jake Hooker

recorded by Joan Jett & The Blackhearts

I saw him dancing there by the record machine.
I knew he must have been about seventeen.
The beat was going strong, playing my favorite song,
And I could tell it wouldn't be long
Till he was with me, yeah, me.
And I could tell it wouldn't be long
Till he was with me, yeah me, singin',

Refrain:
"I love rock 'n roll,
So put another dime in the jukebox, baby.
I love rock 'n roll,
So come and take your time and dance with me."

He smiled, so I got up and asked for his name.
"That don't matter," he said, "cause it's all the same."
I said, "Can I take you home where we can be alone?"
And next, we were moving on,
And he was with me, yeah, me.
And next we were moving on,
And he was with me, yeah, me, singin',

Refrain

I said, "Can I take you home where we can be alone?"
Next we were moving on,
And he was with me, yeah, me.
And we'll be moving on
And singin' that same old song, yeah, with me, singin',

Refrain

If You Love Somebody Set Them Free

Music and Lyrics by Sting

recorded by Sting

Free, free, set them free.
Free, free, set them free.
If you need somebody, call my name.
If you want someone, you can do the same.
If you want to keep something precious,
Got to lock it up and throw away the key.
You want to hold on to your possessions,
Don't even think about me.

Refrain:
If you love somebody, If you love someone,
If you love somebody, If you love someone,
Set them free.

If it's a mirror you want, just look into my eyes,
Or a whipping boy, someone to despise.
Or a prisoner in the dark
Tied up in chains you just can't see,
Or a beast in a gilded cage;
That's all some people ever want to be.

Refrain

You can't control an independent heart,
(Can't love what you can't keep.)
Can't tear the one you love apart.
(Can't love what you can't keep.)
Forever conditioned to believe we can't live,
We can't live here and be happy with less.
With so many riches, so many souls,
With everything we see that we want to possess.

Repeat Verse 1

Refrain

Jack and Diane

Words and Music by John Mellencamp

recorded by John Cougar

A little ditty about Jack and Diane,
Spoken: Two American kids growin' up in the heartland.
Sung: Jack, he's gonna be a football star.
Spoken: Diane's debutante back seat of Jacky's car.

Sung: Suckin' on a chili dog outside the Tastee Freeze;
Spoken: Diane sittin' on Jacky's lap. He's got his hands
  between her knees.
Jack, he says, "Hey, Diane, let's run off behind a shady tree;
Dribble off those Bobbie Brooks. Let me do what I please."

Refrain, sung:
O yeah, life goes on,
Long after the thrill of living is gone.
Oh yeah, life goes on,
Long after the thrill of living is gone.
Spoken: Now, walk on.

Sung: Jack, he sits back, collects his thoughts for a moment;
Spoken: Scratches his head and does his best James Dean.
"Well, then, there, Diane, we gotta run off to the city."
Diane says, "Baby, you ain't missin' a thing."

Refrain

Oh, let it rock, let it roll,
Let the Bible Belt come and save my soul;.
Holdin' on to sixteen as long as you can;
Change is comin' 'round real soon, make us women and men.

Refrain

A little ditty about Jack and Diane,
Spoken: Two American kids doin' the best that they can.

Jessie's Girl

Words and Music by Rick Springfield

recorded by Rick Springfield

Jessie is a friend;
Yeah, I know he's been a good friend of mine.
But lately something's changed; it ain't hard to define:
Jessie's got himself a girl and I wanna make her mine.

And she's watchin' him with those eyes,
And she's lovin' him with that body, I just know it!
Yeah and he's holdin' her in his arms late, late at night.
You know I wish that I had Jessie's girl.
I wish that I had Jessie's girl.
Where can I find a woman like that?

I'll play along with the charade;
There doesn't seem to be a reason to change.
You know, I feel so dirty when they start talkin' cute;
I wanna tell her that I love her, but the point is prob'ly moot.

And she's watchin' him with those eyes,
And she's lovin' him with that body, I just know it!
Yeah and he's holdin' her in his arms late, late at night.
You know I wish that I had Jessie's girl.
I wish that I had Jessie's girl.
Where can I find a woman like that?

Like Jessie's girl, I wish that I had Jessie's girl.
Where can I find a woman,
Where can I find a woman like that?

And I look in the mirror all the time
Wondrin' what she don't see in me.
Yeah, I'm actin' funny and cool with the lines,
Ain't that the way that's supposed to be?

Tell me where can I find a woman like that?
You know I wish that I had Jessie's girl.
I wish that I had Jessie's girl. I want Jessie's girl.
Where can I find a woman like that?

Like Jessie's girl.
I wish that I had Jessie's girl.
I want Jessie's girl.

Just Once

Words by Cynthia Weil
Music by Barry Mann

recorded by Quincy Jones featuring James Ingram

I did my best,
But I guess my best wasn't good enough
'Cause here we are, back where we were before.
Seems nothing ever changes,
We're back to being strangers,
Wondering if we ought to stay
Or head on out the door.

Just once,
Can't we figure out what we keep doing wrong;
Why we never last for very long.
What are we doing wrong?

Just once,
Can't we find a way to finally make it right;
To make magic last for more than just one night?
If we could just get to it, I know we could break through it.

I gave my all,
But I think my all may have been too much;
'Cause Lord knows we're not getting anywhere.
It seems we're always blowin'
Whatever we've got goin'.
And it seems at times, with all we've got,
We haven't got a prayer.

Just once,
Can't we figure out what we keep doing wrong;
Why the good times never last for very long?
Where are we goin' wrong?

Just once,
Can't we find a way to finally make it right?
To make the magic last for more than just one night?
I know we could get through it, if we could just get to it.

Just once,
I want to understand;
Why it always comes back to goodbye.
Why can't we get ourselves in hand,
And admit to one another
We're no good without each other.
Take the best and make it better.
Find a way to stay together.

Just once,
Can't we find a way to finally make it right;
Oh, to make the magic last for more than just one night?
I know we could break through it,
If we could just get to it, just once.
Whoa, we can get to it, just once.

Just the Two of Us

Words and Music by Ralph MacDonald, William Salter and Bill Withers

recorded by Grover Washington Jr. with Bill Withers

I see the crystal raindrops fall,
And the beauty of it all
Is when the sun comes shining through
To make those rainbows in my mind,
When I think of you sometime,
And I want to spend some time with you.

Refrain:
Just the two of us,
We can make it if we try.
Just the two of us, (just the two of us.)
Just the two of us
Building castles in the sky.
Just the two of us, you and I.

We look for love; no time for tears.
Wasted water's all that is
And it don't make no flowers grow.
Good things might come to those who wait
But not for those who wait too late.
We've got to go for all we know.

Refrain

I see the crystal raindrops fall,
On the window down the hall,
And it becomes the morning dew.
And darling, when the morning comes
And I see the morning sun
I want to be the one with you.

Refrain

Keep On Loving You

Words and Music by Kevin Cronin

recorded by R.E.O. Speedwagon

You should have seen by the look in my eyes, baby,
There was somethin' missin'.
You should have known by the tone of my voice, maybe,
But you didn't listen.
You played dead, but you never bled.
Instead you laid still in the grass
All coiled up and hissin'.

And though I know all about those men,
Still I don't remember.
'Cause it was us, baby, way before them,
And we're still together.

Refrain:
And I meant every word I said.
When I said that I love you
I meant that I'll love you forever.
And I'm gonna keep on lovin' you,
'Cause it's the only thing I wanna do.
I don't wanna sleep. I just wanna keep on lovin' you.

Repeat refrain

Baby, I'm gonna keep on lovin' you,
'Cause it's the only thing I wanna do.
I don't wanna sleep. I just wanna keep on lovin' you.

Kiss on My List

Words and Music by Janna Allen and Daryl Hall

recorded by Hall & Oates

My friends wonder why I call you all the time; what can I say?
I don't feel the need to give such secrets away.
You think maybe I need help; no, I know I'm right, all right.
I'm just better off not listening to friends' advice.
When they insist on knowing my bliss, I tell them this.
When they want to know what the reason is,
I only smile when I lie, then I tell them why:

Refrain:
Because your kiss, your kiss is on my list,
Because your kiss, your kiss is on my list,
Because your kiss is on my list of the best things in life.
Because your kiss is on my list,
Because your kiss, your kiss I can't resist,
Because your kiss is what I miss when I turn out the light.

I go crazy wondering what there is to really see.
Did the night just take up your time 'cause it means more to me?
Sometimes I forget what I'm doing, I don't forget what I want, I want.
Regret what I've done, regret you? I couldn't go on.
But if you insist on knowing my bliss, I'll tell you this.
If you want to know what the reason is,
I'll only smile when I lie, then I'll tell you why:

Refrain

Kissing a Fool

Words and Music by George Michael

recorded by George Michael

You are far when I could have been your star.
You listened to people,
Who scared you to death and from my heart.
Strange that you were strong enough to even make a start,
But you'll never find peace of mind till you listen to your heart.

People, you can never change the way they feel,
Better let them do just what they will, for they will
If you let them steal your heart from you.
People, will always make a lover feel a fool,
But you know I love you

We could have shown them all,
We should have seen love through.
Fooled me with the tears in your eyes,
Covered me with kisses and lies,
So goodbye, eye, eye, eye, eye,
But please don't take my heart.

You are far, I'm never gonna be your star.
I'll pick up the pieces and mend my heart.
Maybe I'll be strong enough, I don't know where to start.
But I'll never find peace of mind while I listen to my heart.

People, you can never change the way they feel.
Better let them do just what they will, for they will
If you let them steal your heart from you.
People will always make a lover feel a fool,
But you knew I loved you.
We could have shown you all,
La, la, la, la, la, la.

But remember this,
Every other kiss that you ever give
Long as we both live.
When you need the hand of another man
One you really can surrender with,
I will wait for you like I always do,
There's something that can't compare
With any other.

You are far when I could have been your star.
You listened to people
Who scared you to death and from my heart.
Strange that I was wrong enough
To think you'd love me too.
Guess you were kissing a fool.
You must have been kissing a fool.

Lady in Red

Words and Music by Chris DeBurgh

recorded by Chris DeBurgh

I've never seen you looking so lovely as you did tonight;
I've never seen you shine so bright.
I've never seen so many men ask you if you wanted to dance.
They're looking for a little romance,
Given half a chance.
I have never seen that dress you're wearing,
Or the highlights in your hair that catch your eyes.
I have been blind.

Refrain:
The lady in red is dancing with me,
Cheek to cheek.
There's nobody here, it's just you and me.
It's where I wanna be.
But I hardly know this beauty by my side.
I'll never forget the way you look tonight.

I've never seen you looking so gorgeous as you did tonight;
I've never seen you shine so bright.
You were amazing.
I've never seen so many people
Want to be there by your side,
And when you turned to me and smiled,
It took my breath away.
I have never had such a feeling,
Such a feeling of complete and utter love
As I do tonight.

Refrain

I never will forget the way you look tonight.
The lady in red.
The lady in red.
The lady in red.
My lady in red.

Spoken: I love you.

Leader of the Band

Words and Music by Dan Fogelberg

recorded by Dan Fogelberg

An only child alone and wild, a cabinet maker's son,
His hands were meant for different work and his heart
   was known to none.
He left his home and went his lone and solitary way,
And he gave to me a gift I know I never can repay.

A quiet man of music denied a simpler fate,
He tried to be a soldier once but his music wouldn't wait.
He earned his love through discipline, a thundering velvet hand.
His gentle means of sculpting souls took me years to understand.

The leader of the band is tired and his eyes are growing old,
But his blood runs through my instrument and his song is in my soul.
My life has been a poor attempt to imitate the man.
I'm just a living legacy to the leader of the band.

My brother's loves were different for they heard another call;
One went to Chicago, and the other to St. Paul.
And I'm in Colorado when I'm not in some hotel,
Living out this life I've chose and come to know so well.

I thank you for the music and your stories of the road.
I thank you for the freedom when it came my time to go.
I thank you for the kindness and the times when you got tough.
And papa, I don't think I said "I love you" near enough.

The leader of the band is tired and his eyes are growing old,
But his blood runs through my instrument and his song is in my soul.
My life has been a poor attempt to imitate the man.
I'm just a living legacy to the leader of the band.
I am the living legacy to the leader of the band.

Legs

Words and Music by Billy F Gibbons, Dusty Hill and Frank Beard

recorded by ZZ Top

She got legs. She knows how to use them.
She never begs. She knows how to choose them.
She holdin' leg, wonderin' how to feel them.
Would you get behind them if you could only find them?
She's my baby, she's my baby. Yeah it's all right. Oh, yeah.

She's got hair down to her fanny.
She's kinda jetset. Try undo her panties.
Every time she's dancin' she knows what to do.
Everybody wants to see, see if she can use it.
She's so fine. She's all mine. Girl, you got it right.

She got legs. She knows how to use them.
She never begs. Knows how to choose them.
She got a dime all of the time.
Stays out at night, movin' through time.
Whoa, I want her. Shit, I got to have her. The girl is all right.
She's all right.

Longer

Words and Music by Dan Fogelberg

recorded by Dan Fogelberg

Longer than there've been fishes in the ocean,
Higher than any bird ever flew,
Longer than there've been stars up in the heavens,
I've been in love with you.

Stronger than any mountain cathedral,
Truer than any tree ever grew,
Deeper than any forest primeval,
I am in love with you.

I'll bring
Fires in the winters;
You'll send
Showers in the springs.
We'll fly
Through the falls and summers
With love on our wings.

Through the years as the fire starts to mellow,
Burning lines in the book of our lives.
Though the binding cracks and pages start to yellow,
I'll be in love with you.
I'll be in love with you

Repeat Verse 1

I am in love with you.

Like a Rock

Words and Music by Bob Seger

recorded by Bob Seger

Stood there boldly,
Sweatin' in the sun.
Felt like million,
Felt like number one.
The height of summer,
I'd never felt that strong,
Like a rock.

I was eighteen,
Didn't have a care.
Workin' for peanuts,
Not a dime to spare,
But I was lean and solid everywhere,
Like a rock.

My hands were steady,
My eyes were clear and bright.
My walk had purpose,
My steps were quick and light,
And I held firm to what I felt was right,
Like a rock.

Like a rock,
I was strong as I could be;
Like a rock,
Nothin' ever got to me;
Like a rock,
I was somethin' to see,
Like a rock.

And I stood arrow straight
unencumbered by the weight
Of all these hustlers and their schemes;
I stood proud, I stood tall, high above it all.
I still believed in my dreams.

Twenty years now;
Where's they go?
Twenty years;
I don't know.
I sit and I wonder sometimes
Where they've gone.

And sometime late at night,
When I'm bathed in the firelight,
The moon comes callin' a ghostly white,
And I recall.

I recall like a rock,
Standin' arrow straight
Like a rock,
Chargin' from the gate
Like a rock,
Carryin' the weight
Like a rock.

Oh, like a rock,
The sun upon my skin
Like a rock,
Hard against the wind
Like a rock,
See myself again
Like a rock.

Like a Virgin

Words and Music by Billy Steinberg and Tom Kelly

recorded by Madonna

I made it through the wilderness.
Somehow I made it through.
Didn't know how lost I was until I found you.
I was beat, incomplete. I'd been had.
I was sad and blue. But you made me feel,
Yeah, you made me feel shiny and new.

Like a virgin, touched for the very first time.
Like a virgin, when your heart beats next to mine.

Gonna give you all my love, boy.
My fear is fadin' fast.
Been savin' it all for you, 'cause only love can last.
You're so fine, and you're mine. Make me strong.
Yeah, you make me bold. Oh, your love thawed out,
Yeah, your love thawed out what was scared and cold.

Like a virgin, touched for the very first time.
Like a virgin, with your heart beat next to mine.
Ooh, ooh, ooh.

You're so fine, and you're mine.
I'll be yours till the end of time.
'Cause you made me feel,
Yeah, you made me feel I've nothing to hide.

Like a virgin, touched for the very first time.
Like a virgin, with your heartbeat next to mine.

Repeat and Fade:
Like a virgin. Ooh, ooh, like a virgin.
Feels so good inside when you hold me
And your heart beats and you love me.

Livin' on a Prayer

Words and Music by Jon Bon Jovi, Richie Sambora and Desmond Child

recorded by Bon Jovi

Tommy used to work on the docks, union's been on strike.
He's down on his luck, it's tough, so tough.
Gina works the diner all day working for her man.
She brings home her pay, for love, for love.
She says:

Refrain:
We've got to hold on to what we've got.
It doesn't make a difference if we make it or not.
We've got each other and that's a lot for love.
We'll give it a shot.
Whoa, we're halfway there.
Whoa, livin' on a prayer.
Take my hand, we'll make it, I swear.
Whoa, livin' on a prayer.

Tommy's got his six string in hock,
Now he's holding in what he used to make it talk.
So tough, it's tough.
Gina dreams of runnin away;
When she cries in the night, Tommy whispers:
Baby, it's O.K. someday.

Refrain

Oh, we've got to hold on, ready or not,
You live for the fight when it's all that you've got.

Repeat and Fade:
Whoa, we're halfway there.
Whoa, livin' on a prayer.
Take my hand and we'll make it, I swear.
Whoa, livin' on a prayer.

Love Is a Battlefield

Words and Music by Mike Chapman and Holly Knight

recorded by Pat Benatar

Refrain:
We are young.
Heartache to heartache we stand;
No promises, no demands.
Love is a battlefield.
We are strong.
No one can tell us we're wrong,
Searching our hearts for so long,
Both of us knowing love is a battlefield.

You're begging me to go, then making me stay.
Why do you hurt me so bad?
It would help me to know, do I stand in your way,
Or am I the best thing you've had?
Believe me, believe me, I can't tell you why,
But I'm trapped by your love and I'm chained to your side.

Refrain

When I'm losing control, will you turn me away
Or touch me deep inside?
And when all this gets old, will it still feel the same?
There's no way this will die.
But if we get much closer I could lose control,
And if your heart surrenders, you'll need me to hold.

Refrain

Morning Train (Nine to Five)

Words and Music by Florrie Palmer

recorded by Sheena Easton

I wake up every morning, I stumble out of bed,
A-stretching and a-yawning, another day appeared.
It seems to last forever and time goes slowly by.
Till Babe and me's together, then it starts to fly.

From the moment Babe is with me time can take a flight.
The moment that he's with me everything's all right.
Night time is the right time we make love.
That is his and my time we take off.

Refrain Twice:
My baby takes the morning train
He works from nine to five and then
He takes another home again
To find me waiting for him.

He takes me to a movie or to a restaurant.
Spoken: Slow dancin'! Sung: Or anything I want.
Only when he's with me I catch a light.
Only what he gives me makes me feel all right.

Refrain Twice

All day I think of him, dreaming of him constantly.
I'm crazy mad for him and he's crazy mad for me.
When he steps off that train amazingly full of fight.
He works all day to earn his pay so we can play all night.

Refrain

Making Love Out of Nothing at All

Words and Music by Jim Steinman

recorded by Air Supply

I know just how to whisper and I know just how to cry;
I know just where to find the answers and I know just how to lie.
I know just how to fake it, and I know just how to scheme;
I know just when to face the truth, and then I know just
  when to dream.
And I know just where to touch you, and I know just what to prove;
I know when to pull you closer, and I know when to let you loose.

And I know the night is fading, and I know that time's gonna fly;
And I'm never gonna tell you everything I've got to tell you,
But I know I've got to give it a try.
And I know the roads to riches, and I know the ways to fame;
I know all the rules and then I know how to break 'em
And I always know the name of the game.

But I don't know how to leave you, and I'll never let you fall;
And I don't know how you do it, making love out of nothing at all;
Out of nothing at all, out of nothing at all, out of nothing at all,
Out of nothing at all, out of nothing at all, out of nothing at all.

Every time I see you all the rays of the sun
Are streaming through the waves in your hair;
And every star in the sky is taking aim at your eyes like a spotlight.
The beating of my heart is a drum,
And it's lost and it's looking for a rhythm like you.
You can take the darkness from the pit of the night
And turn into a beacon burning endlessly bright.
I've got to follow it, 'cause everything I know,
Well it's nothing till I give it you.

I can make the run or stumble. I can make the final block.
And I can make every tackle at the sound of the whistle
I can make all the stadiums rock.
I can make tonight forever, or I can make it disappear by the dawn.
And I can make you every promise that has ever been made
And I can make all your demons be gone.
But I'm never gonna make it without you.
Do you really wanna see me crawl?

And I'm never gonna make it like you do,
Making love out of nothing at all, out of nothing at all,
Out of nothing at all, out of nothing at all.
Out of nothing at all, out of nothing at all.

Maneater

Words by Sara Allen, Daryl Hall and John Oates
Music by Daryl Hall and John Oates

recorded by Hall & Oates

She'll only come out at night,
The lean and hungry type.
Nothing is new, I've seen her here before.
Watching and waiting, oo, she's sitting with you,
But her eyes are on the door.

So many have paid to see
What you think you're getting for free.
The woman is wild,
A she-cat tamed by the purr of a Jaguar.
Money's the matter.
If you're in it for love,
You ain't gonna get too far.

Oh, here she comes,
Watch out, boy, she'll chew you up.
Oh, here she comes. She's a maneater.
Oh, here she comes,
Watch out, boy, she'll chew you up.
Oh, here she comes. She's a maneater.

I wouldn't if I were you;
I know what she can do.
She's deadly, man;
She could really rip your world apart.
Mind over matter.
Oo, the beauty is there.
But a beast is in the heart.

Oo, hoo.

Repeat and Fade:
Oh, here she comes. Here she comes.
Watch out, boy, she'll chew you up.
Oh, here she comes, She's a maneater.
Oh, here she comes, oh, she'll chew you up.
Oh, here she comes.
Here she comes, she's a maneater.

Material Girl

Words and Music by Peter Brown and Robert Rans

recorded by Madonna

Some boys kiss me, some boys hug me.
I think they're O.K.
If they don't give me proper credit,
I just walk away.

They can beg and they can plead,
But they can't see the light, that's right.
'Cause the boy with the cold hard cash
Is always Mister Right

Refrain:
'Cause we are living in a material world
And I am a material girl.
You know that we are living in a material world
And I am a material girl.

Some boys romance, some boys slow dance.
That's all right with me.
If they can't raise my int'rest then
I have to let them be.

Some boys try and some boys lie
And I don't let them play.
Only boys who save their pennies
Make my rainy day.

Refrain

Living in a material world. (Material.)
Living in a material world.
Living in a material world. (Material.)
Living in a material world.

Boys may come and boys may go
And that's all right, you see.
Experience has made me rich
And now they're after me.

Refrain

A material, a material, a material, a material world.
Living in a material world. (Material.)
Living in a material world.
Living in a material world. (Material.)
Living in a material world.

Midnight Blue

Words and Music by Lou Gramm and Bruce Turgon

recorded by Lou Gramm

Ain't got no regrets.
I ain't losin' track of what way I'm goin'.
I ain't gonna double back, no.
Don't want a misplay, put on no display.
An angel, no, but I know my way.

I used to follow, yeah, that true.
But my followin' days are over,
Now I just gotta follow through.
And I remember when my father said,
He said, "Son, life is simple,
It's either cherry red or midnight blue."
Oh. Midnight blue, oh whoa.

You were the restless one and you did not care
That I was the troubled boy lookin' for a double dare.
I won't apologize for the things I've done and said,
But when I win your heart I'm gonna paint it cherry red.

I don't wanna talk about it.
What you do to me, I can't live without it.
And you might think that it's much too soon
For us to go this far, into the midnight blue.
Oh. It's midnight blue, oh whoa.

If things could be different that'd be a shame,
'Cause I'm the one who can feel the sun
Right in the pourin' rain.
I won't say where and I don't know when
But soon there gonna come a day baby,
I'll be back again.

Yeah, I'll be back for you.
You see, I'm savin' up my love.
Midnight blue, oh. Midnight blue, oh whoa.

Repeat and Fade:
Midnight blue, oh. Midnight blue, oh whoa.

Missing You

Words and Music by John Waite, Charles Sanford and Mark Leonard

recorded by John Waite

Missing you. Missing you.

Every time I think of you,
I always catch my breath.
And I'm still standing here,
And you're miles away,
And I'm wonderin' why you left.

And there's a storm that's ragin'
Through my frozen heart tonight.
I hear your name
In certain circles,
And it always makes me smile.
I spend my time
Thinkin' about you,
And it's almost drivin' me wild.
And there's a heart that's breakin'
Down this long distance line tonight.

I ain't missin' you at all
Since you've been gone away.
I ain't missin' you,
No matter what I might say.

There's a message in the wire,
And I'm sending you this signal tonight.
You don't know how desperate I've become,
And it looks like I'm losin' this fight.

In your world I have no meaning,
Though I'm trying hard to understand.
And it's my heart that's breakin'
Down this long distance line tonight.

I ain't missin' you at all
Since you've been gone away.
I ain't missin' you,
No matter what my friends say.

And there's a message that I'm sendin' out,
Like a telegraph to your soul.
And if I can't bridge this distance,
Stop this heartbreak overload.
And…

I ain't missin' you at all
Since you've been gone away.
I ain't missin' you,
No matter what my friends say.

Money for Nothing

Words and Music by Mark Knopfler and Sting

recorded by Dire Straits

I want my, I want my MTV.
Now, look at them yo-yos, that's the way you do it,
You play the guitar on the MTV.
That ain't workin', that's the way you do it,
Money for nothin' and your chicks for free.
Now, that ain't workin', that's the way you do it,
Lemme tell ya, them guys ain't dumb.
You maybe get a blister on your little finger,
Maybe get a blister on your thumb.

Refrain:
We gotta install microwave ovens,
Custom kitchen deliveries.
We gotta move these refrigerators,
We gotta move these color TVs.

That little faggot with the earring and the makeup,
Yeah, buddy, that's his own hair.
That little faggot got his own jet airplane.
That little faggot, he's a millionaire.

Refrain Twice

I shoulda learned to play the guitar,
I shoulda learned to play them drums.
Look at that mama, she got it.
Stickin' in the camera, man,
We could have some.

And he's up there. What's that? Hawaiian noises?
He's bangin' on the bongos like a chimpanzee.
Oh, that ain't workin', that's the way you do it,
Get your money for nothin', get your chicks for free.

Refrain

Now, that ain't workin', that's the way you do it,
You play the guitar on the MTV.
That ain't workin', that's the way you do it,
Money for nothin' and your chicks for free.
Money for nothin', and chicks for free.
Get your money for nothin' and your chicks for free.

Repeat and Fade:
Get your money for nothin' and your chicks for free.
I want my, I want my, I want my MTV.

My Prerogative

Words and Music by Bobby Brown, Gene Griffin and Edward Riley

recorded by Bobby Brown

Refrain:
Everybody's talking all this stuff about me.
Why don't they just let me live?
I don't need permission, make my own decisions,
That's my prerogative.

They say I'm crazy. I really don't care.
That's my prerogative.
They say I'm nasty, but I don't give a damn.
Getting girls is how I live.

Some ask me questions. Why am I so real?
But they don't understand me,
Or really don't know the deal about the brother,
Trying hard to make it right.
Not long ago, before I won this fight.
Spoken: Sing.

Refrain

It's my prerogative.
It's my prerogative.
It's the way that I wanna live.
It's my prerogative.

I can do what I feel, it's my prerogative.
No one can tell me what to do.
It's my prerogative,
Spoken: 'Cause what I'm doing I'm doing for you.

Sung:
Don't get me wrong, I'm really not souped,
Ego trips is not my thing.
All these strange relationships really get me down.
I see nothing wrong in spreading myself around.

Refrain

It's my prerogative.
It's my prerogative.
I can do what I wanna do.
It's my prerogative.

I can live my life.
It's my prerogative,
And I'm doing it just for you.
It's my prerogative.

Tell me, tell me why can't I live my life,
Live my life without all of the things that people say.
Oh. *Spoken:* Yo, Teddy, kick it like this.
Sung: Oh no no. I can do what I wanna do.
Me and you together, together, together,
Together, together.

Refrain

The Next Time I Fall

Words and Music by Paul Gordon and Bobby Caldwell

recorded by Peter Cetera with Amy Grant

Love, like a road that never ends.
How it leads me back again
To heartache,
I'll never understand.
Darling, I put my heart upon the shelf
'Til the moment was right. And I tell myself

Refrain:
Next time I fall in love
I'll know better what to do.
Next time I fall in love,
Ooh, Ooh, Ooh.
The next time I fall in love,
The next time I fall in love
It will be with you.

Oh, now, as I look into your eyes,
Well, I wonder if it's wise
To hold you like I've wanted to before.
Tonight, ooh, I was thinking that you might
Be the one who breathes life in this heart of mine.

Refrain

(It will be with you.)
Next time I'm gonna follow through.
And if it drives me crazy,
I will know better why
The next time I try.

Refrain Twice

On the Wings of Love

Words and Music by Jeffrey Osborne and Peter Schless

recorded by Jeffrey Osborne

Just smile for me and let the day begin.
You are the sunshine that lights my heart within.
And I'm sure that you're an angel in disguise.
Come take my hand and together we will ride.

Refrain:
On the wings of love, up and above the clouds;
The only way to fly is on the wings of love.
On the wings of love,
Only the two of us together flying high.

You look at me and I begin to melt,
Just like the snow, when a ray of sun is felt.
And I'm crazy 'bout you, baby, can't you see?
I'd be so delighted if you would come with me.

Refrain

Yes, you belong to me, and I'm yours exclusively.
And right now we live and breathe together.
Inseparable it seems, we're flowing like a stream running free.
Traveling on the wings of love.

Refrain

Together flying high.

Refrain

Flying high upon the wings of love, of love.

Once Bitten Twice Shy

Words and Music by Ian Hunter

recorded by Great White

Well the times are getting hard for you little girl.
I'm a-hummin' and a-strummin' all over God's world.
You can't remember when you got your last meal
And you don't know just how a woman feels.
You didn't know what rock 'n' roll was
Until you met my drummer on a grey tour bus.
I got there in the nick of time
Before he got his hands across your state line. Yeah.

Now it's the middle of the night on the open road.
The heater don't work and it's oh so cold.
You're lookin' tired, and you're lookin' kind-a beat,
The rhythm of the street sure knocks you off your feet.
You didn't know how rock 'n' roll looked
Until you caught your sister with the guys from the group.
Halfway home in the parking lot,
By the look in her eye she was giving what she got.

Refrain:
I said my, my, my. Once bitten, twice shy, babe.
My, my, my. I'm once bitten, twice shy, baby.
My, my, my. I'm once bitten, twice shy, baby.

Oh, woman you're a mess, gonna die in your sleep,
There's blood on my amp and my Les Paul's beat.
Can't keep you home, you're messin' around.
My best friend told me you're the best lick in town.
You didn't know that rock 'n' roll burned
So you bought a candle and you lived and you learned.
You got the rhythm, you got the speed,
Mama's little baby likes it short and sweet.

Refrain

I didn't know you had a rock 'n' roll record
Until I saw your picture on another guy's jacket.
You told me I was the only one
But look at you now it's dark and is dawn.

I said oh my, my, my. once bitten, twice shy, babe.
My, my, my. I'm once bitten, twice shy, baby.
My, my, my. I'm once bitten, twice shy, babe.
My, my, my. I'm once bitten, twice shy.
Oh, so shy.

One Moment in Time

Words and Music by Albert Hammond and John Bettis

recorded by Whitney Houston

Each day I live, I want to be
A day to give the best of me.
I'm only one, but not alone.
My finest day is yet unknown.

I broke my heart for every gain.
To taste the sweet, I faced the pain.
I rise and fall, yet through it all
This much remains:

Refrain:
I want one moment in time
When I'm more than I thought I could be,
When all of my dreams are a heartbeat away
And the answers are all up to me.
Give me one moment in time
When I'm racing with destiny.
Then, in that one moment in time,
I will feel, I will feel eternity.

I've lived to be the very best.
I want it all, not time for less.
I've laid the plans,
Now lay the chance here in my hands.

Refrain

You're a winner for a lifetime
If you seize that one moment in time,
Make it shine.

Give me one moment in time
When I'm more than I thought I could be,
When all of my dreams are a heartbeat away
And the answers are all up to me.
Give me one moment in time
When I'm racing with destiny.
Then, in that one moment in time,
I will be, I will be, I will be free.
I will be free.

One More Night

Words and Music by Phil Collins

recorded by Phil Collins

I've been trying for so long
To let you know,
Let you know how I feel,
And if I stumble, if I fall
Just help me back,
So I can make you see.

Please give me one more night,
Give me one more night.
One more night,
'Cause I can't wait forever.
Give me just one more night,
Oh, just one more night,
Oh, one more night,
'Cause I can't wait forever.

I've been sitting here so long
Wasting time,
Just staring at the phone,
And I was wondering, should I call you?
Then I thought,
Maybe you're not alone.

Please give me one more night,
Give me just one more night,
One more night.
'Cause I can't wait forever.
Please give me one more night,
Oh, just one more night,
Oh, one more night,
'Cause I can't wait forever.

Refrain:
Give me one more night,
Give me just one more night,
Just one more night
'Cause I can't wait forever.

Like a river to the sea,
I will always be with you,
And if you sail away
I will follow you.

Refrain

I know there'll never be a time
You'll ever feel the same,
And I know it's only right.
But if you change your mind,
You know that I'll be here,
And maybe we both can learn.

Give me just one more night,
Give me just one more night.
One more night,
'Cause I can't wait forever.
Give me just one more night,
Give me just one more night,
Oh, one more night,
'Cause I can't wait forever.

Ooh, ooh, ooh...

Owner of a Lonely Heart

Words and Music by Trevor Horn, Jon Anderson, Trevor Rabin and Chris Squire

recorded by Yes

Move yourself.
You always live your life
Never thinking of the future.
Prove yourself.
You are the move you make.
Take your chances, win or loser.
See yourself.
You are the steps you take.
You and you, and that's the only way.
Shake, shake yourself.
You're every move you make.
So the story goes.

Refrain:
Owner of a lonely heart.
Owner of a lonely heart.
(Much better than a)
Owner of a broken heart.
Owner of a lonely heart.
Say you don't want to change it.
You've been hurt so before.

Watch it now,
The eagle in the sky,
How he dancin' one and only.
You lose yourself.
No, not for pity's sake.
There's no real reason to be lonely.
Be yourself.
Give your free will a chance.
You've got to want to succeed.

Refrain

After my own indecision,
They confused me so.
My love said never question your will at all.
In the end you've got to go.
Look before you leap
And don't you hesitate at all. No, no.

Refrain Twice

Sooner or later each conclusion
Will decide the lonely heart.
(Owner of a lonely heart.)
It will excite it,
Will delight it,
Will give a better start.
(Owner of a lonely heart.)
Don't deceive your free will at all.

Twice:
Don't deceive your free will at all.
Don't deceive your free will at all.
Just receive it.
Just receive it.

Photograph

Words and Music by Joe Elliott, Steve Clark, Peter Willis,
Richard Savage, Richard Allen and Robert Lange

recorded by Def Leppard

Ooh! I'm out-ta luck, out-ta love.
Got a photograph picture of.
Passion killer, you're too much.
You're the only one I wanna touch.

I see your face every time I dream,
On every page, every magazine.
So wild and free, so far from me.
You're all I want, my fantasy, yeah.

Oh! Look what you've done to this rock and roll clown.
Oh! Look what you've done.
Photograph, I don't want your photograph.
I don't need your photograph.
All I've got is a photograph, but it's not enough.

I'd be your lover if you were there.
Put your hurt on me if you dare.
Such a woman, you got style.
You make every man feel like a child.

You got some kinda hold on me.
You're all wrapped up in mystery.
So wild and free, so far from me.
You're all I want, my fantasy, yeah.

Oh! Look what you've done to this rock and roll clown.
Oh! Look what you've done. I'm glad I love you.
Photograph, I don't want your photograph.
I don't need your photograph.
All I've got is a photograph.
You've gone straight to my head.

Oh! Look what you've done to this rock and roll clown.
Oh! Look what you've done. I'm glad I love you.
Photograph, I don't want your photograph.
I don't need your photograph.
All I've got is a photograph.
I wanna touch you.

Repeat and Fade:
Oh! Photograph. Photograph. Photograph. Photograph.

Physical

Words and Music by Stephen A. Kipner and Terry Shaddick

recorded by Olivia Newton-John

I'm sayin' all the things that I know you'll like,
Makin' good conversation,
And I gotta handle you just right,
You know what I mean.
I took you to an intimate restaurant,
Then to a suggestive movie,
There's nothing left to talk about
'Less it's horizontally.

Let's get physical, physical,
I wanna get physical, let's get into physical.
Let me hear your body talk, your body talk,
Let me hear your body talk.
Let's get physical, physical,
I wanna get physical, let's get into physical.
Let me hear your body talk, your body talk,
Let me hear your body talk.

I've been patient, I've been good,
Try'n to keep my hands on the table,
It's gettin' hard this holdin' back,
You know what I mean.
I'm sure you'll understand my point of view,
We know each other mentally,
You've gotta know that you're bringin' out
The animal in me.

Let's get physical, physical,
I wanna get physical, let's get into physical.
Let me hear your body talk, your body talk,
Let me hear your body talk.
Let's get animal, animal,
I wanna get animal, let's get into animal.
Let me hear your body talk, your body talk,
Let me hear your body talk.

Let's get physical, physical,
I wanna get physical, let's get into physical.
Let me hear your body talk, your body talk,
Let me hear your body talk.
Let's get physical, physical,
I wanna get physical, let's get into physical.
Let me hear your body talk, your body talk,
Let me hear your body talk.

Repeat and Fade:
Let me hear your body talk,
Let me hear your body talk.

Rapture

Words and Music by Deborah Harry and Chris Stein

recorded by Blondie

Toe to toe dancing very close,
Body breathing almost comatose.
Wall to wall people hypnotized,
And they're stepping lightly,
Hang each night in rapture.

Back to back sacroiliac,
Spineless movement and a wild attack.
Face to face sightless solitude,
And it's finger popping,
Twenty-four hour shopping in rapture.

Rap 1:
Fab five Freddy told me everybody's fly,
D.J. spinnin' I said, "My, my."
Flash is fast, flash is cool,
Francois, c'est pas flache non due.
And you don't stop, sure shot.
Go out to the parking lot and
Get in your car and drive real far.
And you drive all night and then you see a light,
And it comes right down and it lands on the ground,
And out comes the man from Mars.
And you try to run but he's got a gun
And he shoots you dead and he eats your head.
And then you're in the man from Mars.
You go out at night eating cars.

You eat Cadillacs, Lincolns too,
Mercuries and Subaru and you don't stop.
You keep on eating cars.
Then when there's no more cars you go out at night
And eat up bars where the people meet
Face to face, dance cheek to cheek,
One to one, man to man.
Dance toe to toe, don't move too slow
'Cause the man from Mars is through with cars,
He's eating bars.
Yeah, wall to wall, door to door,
Hall to hall he's gonna eat 'em all.
Rapture be pure, take a tour
Through the sewer.
Don't strain your brain, paint a train.
You'll be singin' in the rain.
I said, "Don't stop, do punk rock."

Rap 2:
Well, now you see what you wanna be
Just have your party on TV
'Cause the man from Mars won't eat up bars
Where the TV's on.
And now he's gone back up to space
Where he won't have a hassle with the human race.
And you hip hop, and you don't stop,
Just blast off. A sure shot,
'Cause the man from Mars stopped eatin' cars
And eatin' bars, and now he only eats guitars.
Get up.

Real Love

Words and Music by Michael McDonald and Patrick Henderson

recorded by The Doobie Brothers

Darlin', I know I'm just another head on your pillow.
If only just tonight, girl, let me hear you lie just a little.
Tell me I'm the only man that you ever really loved.
Honey, take me back in my memory place when it was all very right,
So very nice, so very nice.

Here, darlin', stands another bandit wanting you.
In and out your life, they come and they go.
Your days and nights like a wheel that turns,
Grindin' down a secret part of you, deep inside your heart,
That nobody knows.

When you say comfort me to anyone who approaches,
Chalkin' up the hurt, you live and you learn.
Well, we've both lived long enough to know,
That we'd trade it all right now for just one minute of real love,
Real love, real love, I need to believe in real love,
Real love, baby, real love, real love, darlin', real love.

When you say comfort me to anyone who approaches,
Chalkin' up the hurt, you live and you learn.
Well, we've both lived long enough to know,
That we'd trade it all right now for just one minute of real love,
Real love, real love, real love, real love.

Repeat and Fade:
Real love, real love.

Red, Red Wine

Words and Music by Neil Diamond

recorded by Neil Diamond

Red, red wine, go to my head
Make me forget that I still need her so
Red, red wine, it's up to you. All I can do, I've done
But mem'ries won't go. No, mem'ries won't go

I'd have thought that with time
Thoughts of her would leave my head
I was wrong, and I find
Just one thing makes me forget

Red, red wine, stay close to me
Don't let me be alone
It's tearing apart
My blue, blue heart

Rock with You

Words and Music by Rod Temperton

recorded by Michael Jackson

Girl, close your eyes;
Let that rhythm get into you.
Don't try to fight it;
There ain't nothing that you can do.

Relax your mind,
Lay back and groove with mine.
You've gotta feel that heat,
And-a we can ride the boogie,
Share that beat of love.

Refrain:
I wanna rock with you, (all night)
Dance you into day. (sunlight)
I wanna rock with you, (all night)
We're gonna rock the night away.

Out on the floor
There ain't nobody there but us
Girl, when you dance
There's magic that must be love.

Just take it slow
'Cause we've got so far to go.
When you feel that heat
And-a we're gonna ride the boogie,
Share that beat of love.

Refrain

And when the groove is dead and gone
You know that love survives, so we rock forever on.
I wanna rock with you, I wanna groove with you.
I wanna rock with you, I wanna groove with you.

Refrain

Roll with It

Words and Music by Will Jennings, Steve Winwood, Eddie Holland, Lamont Dozier
and Brian Holland

recorded by Steve Winwood

When life is too much, roll with it, baby.
Don't stop and lose your touch, oh no, baby.
Hard time knocking at your door,
I'll tell them you ain't there no more.
Get on through it, roll with it, baby.

Luck'll come and then slip away,
You've got a move, bring it back to stay.
You just roll with it, baby;
Come on and just roll with it, baby, you and me.
Roll with it, baby;
Hang on and just roll with it, baby, hey.

The way that you love is good as money.
I swear by stars above, sweet as honey.
People think you're down and out,
You show them what it's all about.
You can make it, roll with it, baby.

When this world turns its back on you,
Hang in and do that sweet thing you do.
You just roll with it, baby;
Come on and just roll with it, baby, you and me.
Roll with it, baby;
Hang on and just roll with it, baby.

Now there'll be a day, you'll get there, baby.
You'll hear the music play, you'll dance, baby.
You'll leave bad times behind,
Nothing but good times on your mind.
You can do it, roll with it, baby.

Then you'll see life will be so nice,
It's just a step up to paradise.
You just roll with it, baby;
Come on and just roll with it, baby, you and me.
Roll with it, baby;
Hang on and just roll with it, baby.

Sad Songs (Say So Much)

Words and Music by Elton John and Bernie Taupin

recorded by Elton John

Guess there are times when we all need to share a little pain
And ironing out the rough spots, is the hardest part when memories
    remain.
And it's times like these when we all need to hear the radio
'Cause from the lips of some old singer we can share the troubles we
    already know.

So turn 'em on, turn 'em on, turn on those sad songs.
When all hope is gone why don't you tune in and turn them on?
They reach into your room, oh, just feel their gentle touch.
When all hope is gone a sad song says so much.

If someone else is sufferin' enough, oh, to write it down
When every single word makes sense, then it's easier to have those
    songs around.
The kick inside is in the line that finally gets to you.
And it feels so good to hurt so bad and suffer just enough to sing the
    blues.

So turn 'em on, turn 'em on, turn on those sad songs.
When all hope is gone why don't you tune in and turn them on?
They reach into your room, oh, just feel their gentle touch.
When all hope is gone a sad song says so much.

Sad songs, they say, sad songs, they say.
Sad songs, they say, sad songs, they say so much.

So turn 'em on, turn 'em on, turn on those sad songs.
When all hope is gone why don't you tune in and turn them on?
They reach into your room, oh, just feel their gentle touch.
When all hope is gone a sad song says so much.
When all hope is gone you know a sad song says so much.
When every little bit of hope is gone you know a sad song says so
    much.

Sailing

Words and Music by Christopher Cross

recorded by Christopher Cross

Well, it's not far down to paradise,
At least it's not for me.
And if the wind is right you can sail away
And find tranquility.
Oh, the canvas can do miracles,
Just you wait and see.

Believe me.
It's not far to never-never-land,
No reason to pretend.
And if the wind is right you can find the joy
Of innocence again.
Oh, the canvas can do miracles,
Just you wait and see.
Believe me.

Refrain:
Sailing,
Takes me away,
To where I've always heard it could be.
Just a dream and the wind to carry me,
And soon I will be free.

Fantasy,
It gets the best of me
When I'm sailing.
All caught up in the reverie,
Every word is a symphony.
Won't you believe me?

Refrain

Well, it's not far back to reality,
At least it's not for me.
And if the wind is right you can sail away,
And find serenity.
Oh, the canvas can do miracles,
Just you wait and see.
Believe me.

Refrain

Saving All My Love for You

Words by Gerry Goffin
Music by Michael Masser

recorded by Whitney Houston

A few stolen moments is all that we share.
You've got your family and they need you there.
Though I try to resist,
Being last on you list,
But no other man's gonna do,
So I'm saving all my love for you.

It's not very easy living all alone.
My friends try and tell me find a man of my own.
But each time I try,
I just break down and cry.
'Cause I'd rather be home feelin' blue,
So I'm saving all my love for you.

You used to tell me we'd run away together;
Love gives you the right to be free.
You said: "Be patient. Just wait a little longer,"
But that's just an old fantasy.
I've got to get ready, just a few minutes more.
Gonna get that old feelin' when you walk through that door.

'Cause tonight is the night for feeling all right.
We'll be making love the whole night through,
So I'm saving my love,
Yes I'm saving my love,
Yes I'm saving all my love for you.

No other woman is gonna love you more.
'Cause tonight is the night that I'm feeling all right.
We'll be making love the whole night through;
So I'm saving all my love,
Yes, I'm saving all my loving,
Yes I'm saving all my love for you.
For you.

Say You, Say Me

Words and Music by Lionel Richie

recorded by Lionel Richie

Refrain:
Say you, say me.
Say it for always.
That's the way it should be.
Say you, say me.
Say it together, naturally.

I had a dream, I had an awesome dream;
People in the park playin' games in the dark.
And what they played was a masquerade.
But from behind the walls of doubt,
A voice was crying out.

Refrain

As we go down life's lonesome highway,
Seems the hardest thing to do is to find a friend or two.
That helping hand, someone who understands.
And when you feel you've lost your way,
You've got someone there to say, "I'll show you."

Refrain

So you think you know the answers. Oh, no.
Well, the whole world's got ya dancin' that's right, I'm tellin' you.
It's time to start believin', oh yes.
Believe in who you are;
You are a shining star.

Refrain

Say it together, naturally.

She's a Beauty

Words and Music by Steven Lukather, David Foster, John Waybill and Bill Spooner

recorded by The Tubes

Step right up and don't be shy
Because you won't believe your eyes.
She's right here behind the glass,
And you're gonna like her
'Cause she's got class.

You can look inside another world,
You get to talk to a pretty girl.
She's everything you dream about,
But don't fall in love.
She's a beauty,
One in a million girls.
She's a beauty.
Why would I lie?
Why would I lie?

You can say anything you like
But you can't touch the merchandise.
She'll give you every pennies worth,
But it will cost you a dollar first.

You can step outside your little world,
You can talk to a pretty girl.
She's everything you dream about,
But don't fall in love.
She's a beauty.
One in a million girls.
She's a beauty.
Why would I lie?
Why would I lie?

Shout

Words and Music by Roland Orzabal and Ian Stanley

recorded by Tears for Fears

Refrain (Twice):
Shout, shout, let it all out.
These are the things I can do without, come on.
I'm talking to you, come on.

In violent times you shouldn't have to sell your soul.
In black and white they really, really ought to know.
Those one track minds that took you for a working boy,
Kiss them goodbye. You shouldn't have to jump for joy.

Refrain Twice

They gave you life and in return
You gave them hell.
As cold as ice, I hope we live to tell the tale,
I hope we live to tell the tale.

Refrain Twice

And when you've taken down your guard
If I could change your mind
I'd really like to break your heart.
I'd really like to shake your heart.

Refrain

Sister Christian

Words and Music by Kelly Keagy

recorded by Night Ranger

Sister Christian, oh, the time has come
And you know that you're the only one to say O.K.
Where you going what you looking for
You know those boys don't want to play no more with you,
It's true.

Refrain:
You're motoring.
What's your price for flight
In finding mister right
You'll be all right tonight.

Babe you know you're growing up so fast
And momma's worrying that you won't last to say let's play.
Sister Christian there's so much in life
Don't you give it up before your time is due,
It's true.

Refrain

Sister Christian, oh, the time has come
And you know that you're the only one to say O.K.
But you're motoring, you're motoring.

Smooth Operator

Words and Music by Helen Adu and Ray St. John

recorded by Sade

Spoken:
He's laughing with another girl and playing with another heart;
Placing high stakes, making hearts ache.
He's loved in seven languages.
Diamond nights and ruby lights high in the sky,
Heaven help him when he falls.

Sung:
Dianomd life, lover boy,
He move in space with minimum waste
And maximum joy.

City lights and business nights,
When you require streetcar desire for higher heights.
No place for beginners or sensitive hearts,
When sentiment is left to chance,
No place to be ending but somewhere to start.

No need to ask he's a smooth operator,
Smooth operator, smooth operator, smooth operator.
Coast to coast, L.A. to Chicago, western male.
Across the north and south to Key Largo, love for sale.

Face to face each classic case,
We shadow box and double cross yet need the chase.
A license to love, insurance to hold,
Melt all your memories and change into gold,
His eyes are like angels but his heart is cold.

Repeat and Fade:
No need to ask he's a smooth operator,
Smooth operator, smooth operator, smooth operator.
Coast to coast, L.A. to Chicago, western male.
Across the north and south to Key Largo, love for sale.

Somewhere out There

Music by Barry Mann and James Horner
Lyric by Cynthia Weil

from *An American Tail*
recorded by Linda Ronstadt & James Ingram

Somewhere out there, beneath the pale moonlight,
Someone's thinkin' of me and loving me tonight.
Somewhere out there, someone's saying a prayer
That we'll find one another in that big somewhere out there.

And even though I know how very far apart we are
It helps to think we might be wishin' on the same bright star.
And when the night wind starts to sing a lonesome lullaby
It helps to think we're sleeping underneath the same big sky.

Somewhere out there, if love can see us through,
Then we'll be together somewhere out there,
Out where dreams come true.

And even though I know how very far apart we are
It helps to think we might be wishin' on the same bright star.
And when the night wind starts to sing a lonesome lullaby
It helps to think we're sleeping underneath the same big sky.

Somewhere out there, love can see us through,
We'll be together somewhere out there,
Out where dreams come true.

Sweet Dreams
Are Made of This

Words and Music by David A. Stewart and Annie Lennox

recorded by The Eurythmics

Refrain:
Sweet dreams are made of this,
Who am I to disagree?
I travel the world
And the seven seas,
Everybody's looking for something.

Some of them want to use you,
Some of them want to get used by you,
Some of them want to abuse you,
Some of them want to be abused.

Refrain

Hold your head up,
Keep your head up, movin' on.
Hold your head up, movin' on.
Keep your head up, movin' on.
Keep your head up, movin' on.
Hold your head up, movin' on.
Keep your head up, movin' on.
Hold-your head up, movin' on,
Keep your head up…

(Just Like) Starting Over

Words and Music by John Lennon

recorded by John Lennon

Our life together is so precious together.
We have grown. We have grown.
Although our love is still special,
Let's take a chance and fly away somewhere alone.

It's been too long since we took the time.
No one's to blame.
I know time flies so quickly!

But when I see you, darlin',
It's like we both are falling in love again.
It'll be just like starting over, starting over.

Every day we used to make it, love.
Why can't we be makin' love nice and easy?
It's time to spread our wings and fly.
Don't let another day go by, my love.
It'll be just like starting over, starting over.

Why don't we take off alone,
Take a trip somewhere far, far away.
We'll be together all alone again,
Like we used to in the early days.
Well, well, darlin'.

It's been too long since we took the time.
No one's to blame.
I know time flies so quickly!
But when I see you, darlin',
It's like we both are falling in love again.
It'll be just like starting over, starting over.

Our life together is so precious together.
We have grown. We have grown.
Although our love is still special,
Let's take a chance and fly away somewhere.

Straight Up

Words and Music by Elliot Wolff

recorded by Paula Abdul

Lost in a dream; I don't know which way to go.
A-let me say if you are all that you seem,
Then baby, I'm movin' way too slow.

I've been fooled before;
Wouldn't like to get my love caught in the slammin' door.
How about some information, please?

Refrain:
Straight up, now tell me,
Do you really wanna love me forever, oh, oh,
Or am I caught in hit and run?
Straight up, now tell me,
Is it gonna be you and me together, oh, oh, oh,
Or are you just havin' fun?

Time's standing still waiting for some small clue.
A-let me tell you how I keep getting chills
When I think your love is true.

Refrain

You are so hard to read.
You play hide and seek with your true intentions.
If you're only playin' games,
I'll just have to say: a b-b-b-bye, b-b-b-b-bye.

Do, do you love me, do you love me, baby?
Do, do you love me, do you love me, a-hey, baby?
Do, do you love me, do you love me, baby?
Do, do you love me, do you love me, a-tell me baby!

I've been fooled before;
Wouldn't like to get my love caught in the slammin' door.
How about some information, please?

Refrain

Take My Breath Away (Love Theme)

Words and Music by Giorgio Moroder and Tom Whitlock

from the Paramount Picture *Top Gun*
recorded by Berlin

Watching every motion
In my foolish lover's game;
On this endless ocean,
Finally lovers know no shame.
Turning and returning
To some secret place inside;
Watching in slow motion
As you turn around and say,
"Take my breath away.
Take my breath away."

Watching, I keep waiting,
Still anticipating love,
Never hesitating
To become the fated ones.
Turning and returning
To some secret place to hide;
Watching in slow motion
As you turn my way and say,
"Take my breath away."

Through the hourglass I saw you.
In time, you slipped away.
When the mirror crashed, I called you
And turned to hear you say,
"If only for today
I am unafraid.
Take my breath away.
Take my breath away."

Watching every motion
In my foolish lover's game;
Haunted by the notion
Somewhere there's a love in flames.
Turning and returning
To some secret place inside;
Watching in slow motion
As you turn to me and say,
"Take my breath away.
My love, take my breath away.
My love, take my breath away."

Talking in Your Sleep

Words and Music by Jimmy Marinos, Wally Palmar, Mike Skill,
   Coz Canler and Peter Solley

recorded by The Romantics

When you close your eyes and you go to sleep
And it's down to the sound of a heartbeat
I can hear the things that you're dreaming about;
When you open up your heart and the truth comes out.

Refrain:
You tell me that you want me,
You tell me that you need me,
You tell me that you love me.
And I know that I'm right,
'Cause I hear it in the night.
I hear the secrets that you keep
When you're talking in your sleep.
I hear the secrets that you keep
When you're talking in your sleep.

When I hold you in my arms at night
Don't you know you're sleeping in a spotlight?
And all your dreams that you keep inside;
You're telling me the secrets that you just can't hide.

Refrain

I hear the secrets that you keep
When you're talking in your sleep.
I hear the secrets that you keep
When you're talking in your sleep.

When you close your eyes and you fall asleep
Everything about you is a mystery.

Refrain

Repeat and Fade:
I hear the secrets that you keep
When you're talking in your sleep.

Tempted

Words and Music by Christopher Difford and Glenn Tilbrook

recorded by Squeeze

I bought a toothbrush, some toothpaste, a flannel for my face,
Pajamas, a hairbrush, new shoes and a case.
I said to my reflection, let's get out of this place.

Past the church and the steeple, the laundry on the hill,
Billboards and the buildings, memories of it still keep
    calling and calling.
But forget it all, I know I will.

Refrain:
Tempted by the fruit of another,
Tempted, but the truth is discovered.
What's been goin' on,
And now that you have gone, there's no other.
Tempted by the fruit of another,
Tempted, but the truth is discovered.

I'm at the carpark, the airport, the baggage carousel,
The people keep on grabbin', ain't wishin' I was well.
I said it's no occasion, it's no story I can tell.

At my bedside empty pockets, a foot without a sock.
Your body gets much closer, I fumble for the clock,
Alarmed by the seduction, I wish that it would stop.

Refrain

I bought a novel, some perfume, a fortune all for you,
But it's not my conscience that hates to be untrue.
I asked of my reflection, tell me what is there to do?

Refrain

Repeat and Fade:
Tempted by the fruit of another,
Tempted, but the truth is discovered.

These Dreams

Words and Music by Martin George Page and Bernie Taupin

recorded by Heart

Spare a little candle, save some light for me;
Figures up ahead moving in the trees.
White skin in linen, perfume on my wrist,
And a full moon that hangs over these dreams in the mist.

Refrain:
These dreams go on when I close my eyes.
Every second of the night I live another life.
These dreams that sleep when it's cold outside;
Every moment I'm awake, the further I'm away.

Is it a cloak and dagger? Could it be spring or fall?
I walk without a cut through a stained glass wall,
Weaker in my eyesight, candle in my grip,
And words that have no form are falling from my lips.

Refrain

There's something out there I can't resist.
I need to hide away from the pain.
There's something out there I can't resist.
The sweetest song is silence that I've ever heard.
Funny how your feet in dreams never touch the earth.
In a wood full of princes freedom is a kiss,
But the prince hides his face from dreams in the mist.

Refrain

Through the Years

Words and Music by Steve Dorff and Marty Panzer

recorded by Kenny Rogers

I can't remember when you weren't there,
When I didn't care for anyone but you,
I swear we've been through everything there is,
Can't imagine anything we've missed.
Can't imagine anything the two of us can't do.

Through the years
You've never let me down,
You've turned my life around.
The sweetest days I've found
I've found with you.

Through the years,
I've never been afraid,
I've loved the life we've made,
And I'm so glad I've stayed
Right here with you

Through the years.
I can't remember what I used to do,
Who I trusted
Who I listened to before.
I swear you've taught me everything I know,
Can't imagine needing someone so.

Through the years,
I've never been afraid,
I've loved the life we've made,
And I'm so glad I've stayed
Right here with you
Through the years.

Time After Time

Words and Music by Cyndi Lauper and Rob Hyman

recorded by Cyndi Lauper

Lyin' in my bed, I hear the clock tick and think of you,
Caught up in circles, confusion is nothing new.
Flash back
Warm nights,
Almost left behind.
Suitcase of memories
Time after time.

Sometimes you picture me;
I'm walking too far ahead.
You're calling to me,
Can't hear what you've said.
Then you say go slow,
I fall behind.
The second hand unwinds.

Refrain (Twice):
If you're lost you can look
And you will find me
Time after time.
If you fall I will catch you
I'll be waiting
Time after time.

After my picture fades
And darkness returned to gray.
Watching through windows,
You're wondering if I'm O.K.
Secrets stolen
From deep inside.
The drum beats out of time.

Refrain

Time after time.

Total Eclipse of the Heart

Words and Music by Jim Steinman

recorded by Bonnie Tyler

Turn around,
Every now and then I get a little bit lonely
And you're never coming around.
Turn around.
Every now and then I get a little bit tired
Of listening to the sound of my tears,
Turn around.
Every now and then I get a little but nervous
That the rest of all the years have gone by.
Turn around.
Every now and then I get a little bit terrified
And then I see the look in your eyes.
Turn around,
Bright eyes.
Every now and then I fall apart.

Turn around,
Every now and then I get a little bit restless
And I dream of something wild.
Turn around.
Every now and then I get a little bit tired
Of listening to the sound of my tears,
Turn around.
Every now and then I get a little bit angry
And I know I've got to get out and cry.
Turn around.
Every now and then I get a little bit terrified
But then I see the look in your eyes.

Turn around,
Bright eyes.
Every now and then I fall apart,
Bright eyes
Every now and then I fall apart.
And I need you now tonight
And I need you more than ever.
And if you only hold me tight,
We'll be holding on forever.
And we'll only be making it right
'Cause we'll never be wrong.
Together we can take it to the end of the line.
Your love is like a shadow on me all of the time.
I don't know what to do
And I'm always in the dark,
We're living in a powder keg
And giving off sparks.

I really need you tonight.
Forever's gonna start tonight.
Forever's gonna start tonight.

Once upon a time
I was falling in love,
But now I'm only falling apart.

There's nothing I can do,
A total eclipse of the heart.
Once upon a time there was light in my life,
But there's only love in the dark.
Nothing I can say,
A total eclipse of the heart.

Turn around
Every now and then
I know you'll never be
The boy you always wanted to be.
Turn around.
But every now and then
I know you'll always be
The only boy who wanted me the way that I am.
Turn around.
Every now and then
I know there's no one in the universe
As magical and wondrous as you.
Turn around.
Every now and then
I know there's nothing any better
There's nothing that I just wouldn't do.

We Are the World

Words and Music by Lionel Richie and Michael Jackson

recorded by USA for Africa

There comes a time when we heed a certain call,
When the world must come together as one.
There are people dying and it's time to lend a hand
To life, the greatest gift of all.

We can't go on pretending day by day
That someone, somewhere will soon make a change.
We are all a part of God's great big family
And the truth, you know, love is all we need.

Refrain:
We are the world, we are the children,
We are the ones to make a brighter day, so let's start giving.
There's a choice we're making, we're saving our own lives,
It's true, we make better days, just you and me.

Send them your heart so they'll know that someone cares
And their lives will be stronger and free.
As God has shown us by turning stone to bread,
So we all must lend a helping hand.

Refrain

When you're down and out, there seems no hope at all,
But if you just believe, there's no way we can fall.
Let us realize that a change will only come
When we stand together as one.

Refrain

Train in Vain

Words and Music by Mick Jones and Joe Strummer

recorded by The Clash

You say you stand by your man.
So, tell me something I don't understand:
You said you loved me, and that's a fact,
And then you left me; said you felt trapped.

Well, some things you can explain away,
But the heartache's in me 'til this day.
You didn't stand by me? No, not at all!
You didn't stand by me? No way!

All the times when we were close.
I'll remember these things the most.
I see all my dreams come tumbling down.
I can't be happy without you around.

So alone I keep the wolves at bay.
And there's only one thing I can say.
You didn't stand by me? No, not at all!
You didn't stand by me? No way!
You must explain why this must be.
Did you lie when you spoke to me?
Did you stand by me? No, not at all!

Now I got a job but it don't pay.
I need new clothes, I need somewhere to stay.
But, without all these things I can do
But without your love I won't make it through.

But you don't understand my point of view.
I suppose there's nothing I can do.
You didn't stand by me? No, not at all!
You didn't stand by me? No way!
You didn't stand by me? No, not at all!

You didn't stand by me? No way!
You must explain why this must be.
Did you lie when you spoke to me?
Did you stand by me?

Repeat and Fade:
Did you stand by me? No, not at all!
Did you stand by me? No way!

True Colors

Words and Music by Billy Steinberg and Tom Kelly

recorded by Cyndi Lauper

You with the sad eyes,
Don't be discouraged.
Oh, I realize
It's hard to take courage.
In a world full of people
You can lose sight of it all,
And the darkness inside you
Makes you feel so small.
But I see

Refrain:
Your true colors, shinin' through.
I see your true colors,
And that's why I love you.
So don't be afraid to let them show.
Your true colors,
True colors are beautiful,
Like a rainbow.

Show me your smile then,
Don't be unhappy.
Can't remember when
I last saw you laughing.
If this world makes you crazy
And you're takin' all you can bear,
Just call me up
Because you know I'll be there.
And I'll see

Such sad eyes.
Take courage now and realize
When this world makes you crazy
And you're takin' all you can bear,
Just call me up
Because you know I'll be there.
And I see

Your true colors, shinin' through.
I see your true colors,
And that's why I love you.
So don't be afraid to let them show.
Your true colors, true colors,
True colors are shinin' through.

I see your true colors,
And that's why I love you.
So don't be afraid, just let them show.
Your true colors, true colors,
True colors are beautiful,
Beautiful like a rainbow.
Show me your colors.
Show me your rainbow.

Up Where We Belong

Words by Will Jennings
Music by Buffy Sainte-Marie and Jack Nitzsche

from the Paramount Picture *An Officer and a Gentleman*
recorded by Joe Cocker & Jennifer Warnes

Who knows what tomorrow brings;
In a world, few hearts survive.
All I know is the way I feel.
When it's real,
I keep it alive.
The road is long.
There are mountains in our way,
But we climb a step every day.

Refrain:
Love lift us up where we belong,
Where the eagle cry
On a mountain high.
Love lift us up where we belong,
Far from the world we know;
Up where the clear winds blow.

Some hang on to "used to be,"
Live their lives looking behind.
All we have is here and now;
All our life, out there to find.
The road is long.
There are mountains in our way,
But we climb them a step every day.

Refrain

Time goes by, no time to cry,
Life's you and I,
Alive,
Today.

Refrain

Walk Like an Egyptian

Words and Music by Liam Sternberg

recorded by Bangles

All the old paintings on the tomb,
They do the sand dance, don't you know.
If they move too quick, (Oh, way, oh).
They're falling down like a domino.
All the bazaar men by the Nile,
They got the money on a bet.
Gold crocodiles, (Oh, way, oh)
They snap their teeth on your cigarette.
Foreign types with the hookah pipes say,
"Way, oh, way, oh, way, oh, way, oh."
Walk like an Egyptian.

The blonde waitresses take their trays.
They spin around and they cross the floor.
They've got the moves. (Oh, way, oh).
You drop your drink, then they bring you more.
All the school kids so sick of books,
They like the punk and the metal band.
Then the buzzer rings, (Oh, way, oh)
They're walkin' like an Egyptian.
All the kids in the marketplace say,
(Way, oh, way, oh, way, oh, way, oh).
Walk like an Egyptian.

Slide your feet up the street, bend your back,
Shift your arm, then you pull it back.
Life's hard, you know, (Oh, way, oh)
So strike a pose on a Cadillac.

If you wanna find all the cops
They're hanging out in the donut shops.
They sing and dance, (Oh, way, oh)
They spin the club, cruise down the block.
All the Japanese with their yen,
The party boys call the Kremlin.
And the Chinese know, (Oh, way, oh)
They walk the line like Egyptians.
All the cops in the donut shop say,
(Way, oh, way, oh, way, oh, way, oh).
Walk like an Egyptian.
Walk like an Egyptian.

Walking on Sunshine

Words and Music by Kimberley Rew

recorded by Katrina and The Waves

I used to think maybe you loved me,
Now baby, I'm sure.
And I just can't wait till the day
When you knock on my door.
Now every time I go for the mailbox,
Gotta hold myself down.
'Cause I just can't wait till you write me
You're coming around.

Refrain:
Now I'm walking on sunshine. Whoa.
I'm walking on sunshine. Whoa.
I'm walking on sunshine. Whoa,
And don't it feel good! Hey!
All right now, and don't it feel good!
Hey! Yeah!

I used to think maybe you loved me,
Now I know that it's true.
And I don't wanna spend my whole life
Just a-waiting for you.
Now I don't want you back for the weekend,
Not back for a day. No, no, no.
I said baby I just want you back,
And I want you to stay.

Refrain

Walking on sunshine.
Walking on sunshine.
I feel alive, I feel a love,
I feel a love that's really real.
I feel alive, I feel a love,
I feel a love that's really real.
I'm on sunshine, baby. Oh, oh, yeah.
I'm on sunshine, baby.

Refrain

Repeat and Fade:
All right now, and don't it feel good!

Wanted Dead or Alive

Words and Music by Jon Bon Jovi and Richie Sambora

recorded by Bon Jovi

It's all the same, only the names will change,
Ev'ry day, it seems we're wasting away.
Another place, where the faces are so cold.
I'd drive all night, just to get back home.

I'm a cowboy, on a steel horse I ride.
I'm wanted, (wanted), dead or alive.
Wanted, (wanted), dead or alive.

Sometimes I sleep, sometimes it's not for days.
The people I meet always go their sep'rate ways.
Sometimes you tell the day by the bottle that you drink
And times when you're alone, all you do is think.

I'm a cowboy, on a steel horse I ride.
I'm wanted, (wanted), dead or alive.
Wanted, (wanted), dead or alive.

I'm a cowboy, on a steel horse I ride.
I'm wanted, (wanted), dead or alive,
And I walk these streets, a loaded six string on my back.
I play for keeps, 'cause I might not make it back.

I been everywhere, still I'm standing tall.
I've seen a million faces and I've rocked them all,
'Cause I'm a cowboy, on a steel horse I ride.
I'm wanted, (wanted,) dead or alive.

'Cause I'm a cowboy. I got the night on my side.
I'm wanted, (wanted,) dead or alive, (dead or alive,)
Dead or alive, dead or alive. I still ride, (I still ride,)
Dead or alive, dead or alive, dead or alive, dead or alive,
Dead or alive.

We Built This City

Words and Music by Bernie Taupin, Martin Page, Dennis Lambert and Peter Wolf

recorded by Starship

We built this city,
We built this city on rock and roll.
Built this city,
We built this city on rock and roll.

Say you don't know me or recognize my face.
Say you don't care who goes to that kind of place.
Knee-deep in the hoopla, sinking in your fight,
Too many runaways eating up the night.

Refrain:
Marconi plays the mamba,
Listen to the radio.
Don't you remember?
We built this city,
We built this city on rock and roll.

We built this city,
We built this city on rock and roll.
Built this city,
We built this city on rock and roll.

Someone always playing corporation games.
Who cares? They're always changing corporation names.
We just want to dance here, someone stole the stage.
The call us irresponsible, write us off the page.

Refrain

Who counts the money underneath the bar?
Who rides the wrecking ball in two rock guitars?
Don't tell us you need us, 'cause we're the ship of fools,
Looking for America calling through your schools.

Refrain

It's just another Sunday in a tired old street.
Police have got the choke-hold,
Oh, oh, oh, but we just lost the beat.

Refrain

We built, we built this city, now.
We built, we built this city.

What I Like About You

Words and Music by Michael Skill, Wally Palamarchuk and James Marinos

recorded by The Romantics

Hey! Uh-huh. Hey! Uh-huh.

What I like about you, you hold me tight.
Tell me I'm the only one, wanna come over tonight.
Yeah!

Refrain:
Keep on whispering in my ear,
Tell me all the things that I wanna hear, 'cause it's true.
That's what I like about you.

What I like about you,
You really know how to dance.
When you go up down, jump around
Think I've found true romance. Yeah!

Refrain

That's what I like about you.
That's what I like about you.

Hey! Uh-huh. Hey! Uh-huh.

What I like about you, you keep me warm at night.
Never wanna let you go, know you make me feel alright.
Yeah!

Refrain

That's what I like about you.
That's what I like about you.

Whisper: That's what I like about you.
That's what I like about, that's what I like about,
That's what I like about you. Sing: Hey!

Uh-huh. Hey! Hey! Hey! Hey!
Uh-huh. Hey! Hey! Hey! Hey!
Uh-huh. Hey! Hey! Hey! Hey!

What's Love Got to Do with It

Words and Music by Terry Britten and Graham Lyle

recorded by Tina Turner

You must understand, though the touch of your hand makes my pulse
    react,
That it's only the thrill of boy meeting girl, opposites attract.
It's physical, only logical.
You must try to ignore that it means more than that.

Refrain:
Oh, oh, what's love got to do, got to do with it?
What's love but a second-hand emotion?
What's love got to do, got to do with it?
Who needs a heart, when a heart can be broken?

It may seem to you that I'm acting confused when you're close to me.
If I tend to look dazed, I read it someplace, I got cause to be.
There's a name for it, there's a phrase that fits.
But whatever the reason, you do it for me.

Refrain

I've been taking on a new direction.
But I have to say I've been thinking about my own protection.
It scares me to feel this way.

Refrain

What's love got to do, got to do with it?
What's love but a sweet old fashioned notion?
What's love got to do, got to do with it?
Who needs a heart when a heart can be broken?

You Give Love a Bad Name

Words and Music by Jon Bon Jovi, Richie Sambora and Desmond Child

recorded by Bon Jovi

An angel's smile is what you sell.
You promise me heaven, then put me through hell.
Chains of love got a hold on me.
When passion's a prison, you can't break free.

Refrain:
Oh you're a loaded gun. Yeah.
Oh, there's nowhere to run.
No one can save me, the damage is done.
Shot through the heart and you're to blame.
You give love a bad name.
I play my part and you play your game.
You give love a bad name,
Hey, you give love a bad name.

You paint your smile on your lips.
Blood red nails on your finger tips.
A school boy's dream, you act so shy.
Your very first kiss was your first kiss goodbye.

Where Do Broken Hearts Go

Words and Music by Chuck Jackson and Frank Wildhorn

recorded by Whitney Houston

I know it's been some time, but there's something on my mind.
You see, I haven't been the same since that cold November day.
We said we needed space, but all we found was an empty place.
And the only thing I learned is that I need you desperately.
So here I am, and can you please tell me,

Refrain:
Oh where do broken hearts go?
Can they find their way home,
Back to the open arms of a love that's waiting there?
And if somebody loves you, won't they always love you?
I look in your eyes and I know that you still care for me.

I've been around enough to know that dreams don't turn to gold,
And that there is no easy way; no, you just can't run away.
And what we had was so much more than we ever had before.
And no matter how I tried, you were always on my mind.

Refrain

And now that I am here with you, I'll never let you go.
I look into your eyes and now I know. Now I know.

Refrain

So here I am, and can you please tell me,
Oh where do broken hearts go? Can they find their way home,
Back to the open arms of a love that's waiting there?
And if somebody loves you, won't they always love you?
I look in your eyes and I know that you still care for me, for me.
You still care for me.

With Every Beat of My Heart

Words and Music by Tommy Faragher, Lotti Golden and Arthur Baker

recorded by Taylor Dane

Whoo, uh, ah, ah, ah, ah.
Uh, hey, yea, yeah.

I'll keep you in closer to the love I know.
I'm ready and willing, getting out of control.
You win and you lose some, but if you stay in the game,
Before you know it, you'll feel the fire,
But don't get burned by the flame.
No. You'll find the answer any day.

Refrain:
With every beat of my heart,
I keep getting closer to you.
Oh, with every beat of my heart,
Now I know we're getting closer to love.
With every beat.
Whoo, ah, ah, ah, yeah. Ah, ah, ah, ah.

Now, I just want to know you more every day,
And now it won't be long till I hear you say, yeah, yeah,
Uh, say that you do, boy. It's just a matter of time.
Oh, before you know it, you'll feel the fire,
And it's burning deep inside.
No. You'll find the answer in his eyes.

Refrain

With every beat of my heart.
I feel you moving closer to me.
Oh, with every beat of my heart, baby,
I know it's becoming reality.
With every beat.
Whoo, ah, ah, ah, yeah, yeah.

Before you know it, you'll feel the fire,
But don't get burned by the flame.
No. You'll find the answer any day.

With every beat of my heart,
I keep getting closer to you.
Oh, with every beat of my heart,
Now I know we're getting closer to love.

Repeat and fade:
With every beat of my heart,
(With every beat of my heart.)
I feel you moving closer to me.
Oh, with every beat of my heart, baby,
I know it's becoming reality.

Woman

Words and Music by John Lennon

recorded by John Lennon

Woman, I can hardly express
My mixed emotions at my thoughtlessness.
After all, I'm forever in your debt.
And, woman, I will try to express
My inner feelings and thankfulness
For showing me the meaning of success.

Ooh, well, well.
Doo doo doo doo doo.
Ooh, well, well.
Doo doo doo doo doo.

Woman, I know you understand
The little child inside the man.
Please remember, my life is in your hands.
And, woman, hold me close to your heart.
However distant, don't keep us apart.
After all, it is written in the stars.

Ooh, well, well.
Doo doo doo doo doo.
Ooh, well, well.
Doo doo doo doo doo.

Woman, please let me explain.
I never meant to cause you sorrow or pain.
So let me tell you
Again and again and again:

Repeat and Fade:
I love you, yeah, yeah,
Now and forever.
I love you, yeah, yeah,
Now and forever.

You Give Good Love

Words and Music by La Forrest "La La" Cope

recorded by Whitney Houston

I found out what I've been missing,
Always on the run.
I've been looking for someone.

Now you're here like you've been before
And you know just what I need.
It took some time for me to see

That you give good love to me, baby, so good.
Take this heart of mine into your hands.
You give good love to me. (You give good love to me.)
It's never too much
Baby, you give good love.

Not ever stopping, I was always searching
For that perfect love,
The kind that girls like me dream of.

Now you're here like you've been before,
And you know just what I need.
It took some time for me to see...

You give good love to me. Baby, so good.
(Baby too much, we'll never be.)
Take this heart of mine into your hands.
You give good love to me. (You give good love to me.)
It's never too much.
Baby, you give good love.

Now I, I can stop looking around.
It's not what this love's all about.
Our love is here to stay, to stay.
Baby, you give good love.

You give good love to me. Baby, so good.
(Baby too much, we'll never be.)
Take this heart of mine into your hands.
You give good love to me. (You give good love to me.)
It's never too much.
Baby, you give good love.